Inquiry and Innovation in the Classroom

Careers in the 21st century are changing, but traditional education methods are not preparing students for these new jobs and demands. In this thought-provoking book, esteemed educator A. J. Juliani describes how we need to modify our classrooms to instill in students the drive for inquiry and innovation that they will need to succeed beyond school doors. Juliani reveals the ways that teachers can use Google's 20% Time, Genius Hour, and Project-Based Learning to make students more creative, inquisitive, engaged in learning, and self-motivated—the kind of people we need to move society forward! He offers easy ways to implement these ideas while meeting the Common Core and still allowing plenty of time for content instruction.

Special features:

- Research on the benefits of inquiry-based learning
- Connections to the Common Core State Standards
- Stories and examples from the field
- Exciting ideas for using 20% Time, Genius Hour, and Project-Based Learning (PBL) at various grade levels
- Tips for preparing parents and administration for your new instruction
- Ideas for expanding your knowledge and continually learning in this area
- Classroom applications for each chapter, including sample projects and resources
- Bonus content with reproducible materials that you can use in your classroom right now, such as student checklists, questions, lessons, and unit plans

As Juliani emphasizes, if we want our students to change the world, we must change our classrooms to foster inquiry and innovation.

A.J. Juliani is a K-12 Technology Staff Developer at Wissahickon School District and the co-founder of the educational thought group "Education Is My Life." He is a popular blogger, consultant, and conference presenter.

Other Eye On Education Books Available from Routledge
(www.routledge.com/eyeoneducation)

From Notepad to iPad
Using Apps and Web Tools to Engage a New Generation of Students
Matthew D. Gillispie

Reinventing Writing
The 9 Tools That Are Changing Writing, Learning, and Living
Vicki Davis

Engaged, Connected, Empowered
Teaching and Learning in the 21st Century
Ben Curran and Neil Wetherbee

Create, Compose, Connect!
Reading, Writing, and Learning with Digital Tools
Jeremy Hyler and Troy Hicks

Teaching the Common Core Speaking and Listening Standards
Strategies and Digital Tools
Kristen Swanson

Authentic Learning Experiences
A Real-World Approach to Project-Based Learning
Dayna Laur

Flipping Your English Class to Reach All Learners
Strategies and Lesson Plans
Troy Cockrum

Writing Behind Every Door
Common Core Writing in the Content Areas
Heather Wolpert-Gawron

Rebuilding Research Writing
Strategies for Sparking Informational Inquiry
Nanci Werner-Burke, Karin Knaus, and Amy Helt DeCamp

Tech Tools for Improving Student Literacy
Hilarie Davis and Bradford Davey

Big Skills for the Common Core
Literacy Strategies for the 6–12 Classroom
Amy Benjamin and Michael Hugelmeyer

Teaching Students to Dig Deeper
The Common Core in Action
Ben Johnson

Inquiry and Innovation in the Classroom

Using 20% Time, Genius Hour, and PBL to Drive Student Success

A.J. Juliani

NEW YORK AND LONDON

First published 2015
by Routledge
711 Third Avenue, New York, NY 10017

and by Routledge
2 Park Square, Milton Park, Abingdon, Oxon OX14 4RN

Routledge is an imprint of the Taylor & Francis Group, an informa business

Library of Congress Cataloging-in-Publication Data

Juliani, A.J.
Inquiry and innovation in the classroom : using 20% time, genius hour, and PBL to drive student success / A.J. Juliani.
pages cm
Includes bibliographical references.
1. Motivation in education. 2. School-to-work transition. I. Title.
LB1065.J75 2014
370.15′4—dc23
2013047554

ISBN: 978-0-415-74315-0 (hbk)
ISBN: 978-0-415-74316-7 (pbk)
ISBN: 978-1-315-81383-7 (ebk)

Typeset in Bembo
by Apex CoVantage, LLC

Printed and bound in the United States of America by Publishers Graphics, LLC on sustainably sourced paper.

Dedication

To Kylie, Tucker, and Baby #3. May you find your purpose, live life with passion, and never stop learning.

Contents

Acknowledgments

There are so many people who helped shaped this book. I first want to thank my wife for supporting me throughout the process, and always challenging me to do great work. My Mom for reading the manuscript in its many phases, and the rest of my family for always supporting the nerd in me.

I work at one of the best schools in the US. My colleagues at Wissahickon are amazing educators who have taught me so much about teaching and learning. Without them I would never have had the confidence to use inquiry in the classroom. Their work continues to foster innovative thinking every day.

Finally, I want to thank the overwhelming support from my 20% Time and Genius Hour colleagues. Building this PLN has stretched my educational boundaries. Learning from this PLN has moved me to action time and time again. To every classroom teacher that gives their students the gift of inquiry-based learning, this book is for you.

Meet the Author

A.J. Juliani is a K-12 Technology Staff Developer at Wissahickon School District. A.J. previously taught middle and high school English. He also coaches football and lacrosse at the middle school level. As a teacher, A.J. strives to make meaningful connections with students and help them find purpose in their learning. He is a certified Microsoft Innovative Educator and Flat Classroom teacher who participates in global projects with students and staff.

In addition to his teaching experience, A.J. is also the co-founder and chief editor of "Education Is My Life." The group of educators has published five eBooks and continues to share best and next practices in education from a variety of perspectives. A.J. has worked with the International Society for Technology in Education (ISTE) as an instructional consultant and has presented at various educational conferences including the ISTE Leadership Forum and The Global Education Conference. A.J. also spends time working as a consultant, writing curriculum, and blogging at AJJULIANI.com.

A.J. lives in suburban Philadelphia with his wife and two children. He has spent time working in Guatemala with Food for the Hungry, as well as South Africa and Swaziland working with the non-profit Swaziland Relief. More than anything, A.J. is someone who truly believes in the "inquiry-driven" education movement. He has kids of his own, and wants them to grow up in a world that values their ideas.

Foreword
George Couros

Est-que je peux aller aux toilettes?

Out of everything that I learned in taking French classes for eight out of my 12 years in my K-12 schooling, this is the one phrase that I will always remember.

Translated it says, "May I go to the bathroom?"

When I think about that question, that was *easily* the question that I asked most in my time as a student in school, whether it was English or French. If you think about it, if school is to spark the curiosity that we hope for ourselves and our future generation, shouldn't our questions start with "why" or "how," not "may I"? That last question is not about thinking deeply or exploring passions, but it is about compliance. How many times do you now ask someone else permission to go to the bathroom? What a weird thing to think about.

Yet we wonder why we see articles like the one in *Newsweek* in 2010 about a "Creativity Crisis." According to the *Newsweek* article, 1500 CEOs were asked what the most important "leadership competency" was that they would look for and "creativity" came in as a clear number one. In the same article though, schools were listed as one of the reasons that children were *not* creative and stated that within schools, "there's no concerted effort to nurture the creativity of all children."[1]

A question that has always driven my own thinking is do people become creative *because* of school, or *in spite* of it?

As most students, I walked out of school having no idea what I wanted to do. What we were told over and over again was that university and college was a way to a better life, and without having any dream other than being an NBA basketball player (which was not happening), I started on the costly endeavor of going to university without having any idea of what I loved. It is a very costly way to "find yourself," even more so now when careers are harder than ever to obtain. Unfortunately, after six years of university I still had no idea of what I loved, only what I was about to do. My post-secondary education was more of a checklist to the next stage of my life than a way to explore my passions. Luckily years into my career, I found my niche and I couldn't imagine doing anything different now, but how different is my story from others? Years and years of time, thousands and thousands of dollars, and I luckily felt that I had found my passion in my third decade on this earth.

I am grateful that I found my passion and every day I leave my house, it is with a spring in my step, but I was a lucky one. As someone who has a career in education, one of my beliefs is to do everything that I can in our schools so that students can find their passion *during* their time in classrooms. How could I have known what I love if I did not have an opportunity to explore different passions without the help of my teachers? School should be a place not where answers go to die, but questions come to life.

So how do we make this happen within the confines of a system that was built to enhance and mirror industrialism? First off, educators need to start seeing themselves as innovators. We can talk about the constraints of testing, the curriculum, poor leadership, and a million other things, but that is pointing the finger away from what we can do ourselves. We ask our students to solve problems all of the time, and we need to model this ourselves. If you think the system doesn't work for your students, then let's start to think different. A.J. does a nice job debunking the myths of a non-traditional classroom but it is up to you to implement them.

Next, we have to start looking at what the world looks like outside of schools and bring that into our classrooms. As much as I hate to say it, Google has a bigger "research and development" budget than any school I know, and when they are openly sharing some of the ways that they not only engage their employees, but also create environments where innovation flourishes: We should pay attention. What great organizations do is develop their people as thinkers, leaders, and "intrapreneurs" who constantly push innovation from within. Can you imagine what your classroom could look like if we adopted that same mindset as educators?

As I read this book and the ideas that A.J. has shared, I felt my head nodding, emphatically thinking, "I wish I went to school now." Not only is it more engaging, but it has the potential to be so much better. In a world where the *only* constant will be change, how do we get students to think of themselves as innovators not only in the future, but today. As any good book on the notion of innovation will often lead to more questions, A.J. has written something that gives great ideas and will push your learning long after.

Nothing different will happen with your students until something different happens for you first. Hopefully "why" and "how" will become the common question starter for our students, as opposed to "may I", no matter the language.

Note

1 http://www.newsweek.com/creativity-crisis-74665

Introduction

Do you ever wonder why some people thrive in school, then fail to succeed in the real world? Or how some struggling students and drop outs go on to become incredibly successful? Often we make the assumption that success in school prepares us for success in life. Yet, there are many stories that show us quite the opposite. Many of our greatest innovators, creators, and business leaders have struggled in our school system. Some have just been bored at the basic rigor and curriculum set forth in most K-12 schools. Others have dropped out altogether, citing the Mark Twain quote: "I will not let school get in the way of my education."

As an educator, parent, and student myself, I believe it's time we learned from our educational history and plan for the 21st century and beyond. Student success has a very different definition than it did twenty years ago, fifty years ago, or a hundred years ago. School has to look and work differently. But this book is not about tearing down our educational system. Instead, it is about building it up! It's about pulling from the best research and examples to drive student success right now. While some of the ideas in this book may seem new to you, they are grounded in time-tested instructional practices. That's the best part about innovation; it comes out of shared ideas and is built up over time.

We are currently sitting at one of the most important crossroads in our educational history. It is the most important time to be in education. And it is the most important time to fight for a better education. Albert Einstein famously said, "If you always do what you always did, you will always get what you always got." Let's get better results by changing what we are doing now.

This book brings inquiry and innovation to the forefront of the educational discussion. Inquiry is the engine that drives innovation. When students are able to be curious, and explore their interests and passions, innovative work happens.

In this book you will learn how to design inquiry-based learning experiences through 20% Time, Genius Hour, and various projects. You'll also learn about the connection between inquiry and innovation through stories and examples in the field. Lastly, you'll see how these types of learning experiences drive student success in the classroom, and outside of school. They supercharge student's abilities and unleash the potential of amazing work to be done while they are still in school.

I wrote this book because I experienced this firsthand as a teacher. In late 2011 I finished reading Dan Pink's book *Drive*. His book explained that extrinsic motivation—the kind that deals with grades and money—can only move a person to do just enough. Yet, intrinsic motivation—the kind that comes from our passions—can move a person to change the world. He wrote: "Control leads to compliance; autonomy leads to engagement." I wanted my students to be engaged, not controlled by the rewards I was providing.

Right after the holiday break I introduced "The 20% Project." Based on Google's own 20 percent policy, students in my class were able to work on whatever they wanted for 20 percent of their class time each week. Many were confused at first. Many were also excited. Most did not know what to do with their free time.

What I saw were students struggling to find a purpose for their learning, when the purpose had always been provided for them. In time, we got past this hurdle, and my students began to learn for themselves. It was a powerful experience, and one I had to share.

Over the next few weeks and months I began to find a community of teachers online who were doing the same thing: giving students a chance to learn what they were passionate about during class. This community of 20% Time and Genius Hour teachers demonstrated how inquiry-based learning experiences moved students to a new type of in-school success.

Many teachers have asked me how to start this type of learning in their class and in their school. This book is for you. Many teachers have also questioned if this type of learning can work in our schools. This book is definitely for them, too.

I wrote this book for any teacher, student, parent, administrator, or person who is curious about 20% Time, Genius Hour, and inquiry-based learning. Each chapter includes a story of learning, research, and resources to support inquiry, and a classroom application section meant to drive students to innovative work. You'll also find bonus content after each chapter that you can use in your classroom right now.

If we want our students to change the world, we'll have to take a good look at how we can change our classrooms to support inquiry and innovation. Get started in Chapter 1, and see how one student became a huge success after realizing good grades didn't magically turn into a good job.

CHAPTER

1

Real Classrooms for a Real World

Google may be the most famous company to have 20% Time, but many other organizations and businesses have used this "inquiry concept" to their advantage. This chapter takes a look at how working in the real world is very similar to this type of project in school. Full of examples and quotes from leaders in business, it shows how a typical student's path in education does not always prepare them to work in the real world. The use of 20% learning time can change that as it provides a structure for students to develop grit and perseverance.

The Recession-Proof Graduate

Charlie Hoehn was the type of student we all hope our kids will become. He had a 3.8 GPA, high SAT and ACT scores, was on the honor roll, and held positions in a number of clubs. This is what Charlie had been told would lead him to success. His parents, teachers, and society as a whole had led him to believe that hard work in school would pay off. But then it didn't.

Three months after college Charlie had been either ignored or rejected by every company he applied to. He joined a generation of students who were struggling to find jobs in the recession. There was no blueprint on how to compete with 35-year-olds who had been laid off and desperately needed a job to support their family and lifestyle. One night he found himself lying on the bathroom floor. Anxiety was building. Depression was close to setting in. It was then he decided to make a change.

Eight months later Charlie had done a complete 180.

In less than a year he had worked with four *New York Times'* best-selling authors, a Hollywood producer, and various entrepreneurs. Billion dollar companies were approaching him with job offers that he was turning down. Charlie no longer needed to send out his resume, the positions were coming to him, and he was so busy he had to turn away work.

What changed in those eight months?

Charlie stopped following the rules he had learned in school out in the real world. School teaches our students: "Your grades show others how motivated you are. Make sure to have your GPA on your resume, and send it out to as many companies as possible."

Instead, Charlie stopped applying to low-level jobs on CareerBuilder, Monster, and Craiglist. He built an online portfolio and started reaching out to people he wanted to work with and learn from. By doing "free work" for these authors and entrepreneurs, Charlie was able to leverage paying jobs for the future, and built up a strong number of testimonials from influential people.

School teaches us that we have to pay our dues: "Don't skip steps or you won't be prepared for the next level or grade."

Charlie paid his dues, tried to get an entry-level job, and there were no takers. Charlie was tempted to go to grad school, but another $100,000 in student loans kept him away. Instead he self-educated in the areas in which he wanted to work. By reading books, blogs, and watching videos online, Charlie was able to be "in the know" on current trends in the market. He found out who were the top people, and ones most likely to need some extra help. Then he taught himself the "in demand skills" that were needed for each of these jobs (video editing, web design, and online marketing).

School teaches us: "Keep your failures quiet. Don't broadcast your ups and downs to the world."

Charlie built a blog to go with an online portfolio. Charlie wrote about his failures to find a job, and what he was going to do to change his luck. His blog helped establish trust with future employers, and enabled him to be "Googleable." When someone googled his name, they found a wealth of resources tailored to jobs he wanted, as well as a story to support his mission and goals.

The story of Charlie Hoehn does not stop there. He went on to write "The Recession-Proof Graduate," which has been downloaded over 150,000 times. He's given two TEDx talks. He helped Tim Ferriss, Ramit Sethi, Tucker Max, and others reach the *New York Times'* bestseller list. He was the Head Developer on the "Negotiate It" iPhone App, and has worked with a dozen best-selling authors to market their books.

Charlie did all of this before age 30. He did all of this by turning his back on what his schooling taught him, and focusing on what would lead him to success in the real world.

Does School Prepare Us for the Real World?

As a parent I'm hoping that my daughter becomes a great learner. Good grades, lots of activities, and strong SAT/ACT scores. I want her to get into the best possible college. This is what most parents hope for their children. The recipe is simple:

Do well in school = Get into a good college

However, that recipe leads to one of our biggest misconceptions:

Get good grades at your college = Get a good job in the real world

What we end up having is parents pushing students to get good grades (not a bad thing), and get into a good college (again not a bad thing), but their child eventually struggles to find a good job . . . much less their dream job.

On the flip side, we also have students that do not have that pressure from home, and rarely see the connection between "what I do in school" prepares me for "what I do in life."

As an 11th grade English teacher, I used to have "reality check" days for my students. The class started off with the students coming and sitting down ready for the lesson. I had a giant question up on the board: "Who do you want to be?"

Students answered this question in a variety of ways. Some chose a person that they admired, some chose a general answer like "famous," but most looked at me and said: "Mr. J, what do you mean?"

If I had asked them, "what do you want to be?" many would have responded with "rich" or "famous" or "a professional athlete," etc. Instead, the question of "who" threw them off. I explained that each of them had the ability to choose their own path to who they will become. Their choices right now mattered.

Then I asked a second question: "What do you see yourself doing 10 years from now? 20 years from now?"

This was a bit more tangible. Students chose everything from "running my own company" to "sitting on a yacht" and even "teaching a high school class" (I was very proud). After much discussion with each other, I turned to the class and said: "So, how are you going to get there?"

Sadly, the most common answer to this question was: "get good grades." Most of my students couldn't think about what was really needed to reach their ten-year dream. And, it wasn't their fault. Our schooling system likes to push kids' thinking to the next logical step. We learn our "A, B, C's" in kindergarten so we can start spelling in first grade. We learn our multiplication tables and division in 2nd grade so we can start fractions in 3rd grade. We learn how to write a 5-paragraph essay in 8th grade so we can write research papers in high school. When do we ever stop our students and allow them to think about the "big picture"? And more importantly, if my 11th grade students in a top-performing school can't conceptualize how they will reach their goals, what about the rest of our students?

The Future of Work

The popular equation I mentioned above does have a missing piece:

Good Grades = Good School = Good Job = ?

The final piece is supposed to be "Good Life." But the notion that we can be rewarded for simply "doing what we are supposed to do" is limited and quickly becoming false. In fact, the whole notion of work is being changed exponentially.

Hod Lipson is a professor at Cornell University. He said at a recent "Future of Work" symposium:

> Machines are better at learning than humans in many different areas. So now the question is, what will they learn and what's the end game?
>
> If you're talking 100 years, there's no doubt in my mind that all jobs will be gone, including creative ones. And 100 years is not far in the future—some of our children will be alive in 100 years.
>
> In a way, we cannot help ourselves. We try to automate every difficult task that we see. It is rooted in the fact that the mantra of engineering has always been to try to alleviate drudgery and increase productivity—that was the good thing to do. That's what we still train our students to do.[1]

The reality our students and children are facing in the next generation is a stark difference from what previous generations have faced. There are many forces at work: globalization, the spread of technology, and the rise of a global middle class. However, maybe the most important factor to consider is the "types" of jobs that will be available.

Many of us know the US Department of Labor prediction that kids in high school will have had 10–14 different jobs by the time they're in their late thirties, and that 65 percent of our grade-school kids will end up in jobs that haven't yet been invented. Other studies show that by 2020, over half of the workforce will be consultants, freelancers, and independent contractors, cobbling out their own careers.[2]

Let's think about that number for a second . . . 65 percent. More than half our students will be in jobs that are yet to be created. New positions for new companies in new markets. My question is:

> What are we doing in school to get students ready for this future of work?

Preparing a Generation for a Different Type of Success

In this new work landscape employees will have to be innovative, resourceful, and resilient. They will also have different measures of being successful. We make it simple in school. Successful students receive an "A." Failing students receive an "F." And those students who are "average" receive a "B," "C," or "D." Every student falls somewhere along the continuum and conversations about "performance" are dictated on these grades. Although research has shown time and time again that this type of extrinsic motivation does not actually improve a student's performance over time, we still cling to an old way of measuring success.

What does work is intrinsic motivation. When students (or anyone for that matter) are able to learn what they want, they are rewarded through the act of gaining knowledge and demonstrating that knowledge. When a student learns a new instrument or sport, they practice because they want to be successful, not because they will get an "A" if they do well. This is the type of success that will also be found in the future workplace.

Bruce Tulgan, author of the book *Not Everyone Gets a Trophy,* recently explained the new reality of the workplace in a *Time Magazine* article:

> Paying your dues, moving up slowly and getting the corner office—that's going away. In 10 years, it will be gone. Instead, success will be defined not by rank or seniority but by getting what matters to you personally.
>
> Companies alresady want more short-term independent contractors and consultants and fewer traditional employees because contractors are cheaper. And seniority matters less and less as time goes on, because it's about the past, not the future.[3]

Companies have to deal with this new future as well. Hiring is a process that has always been seen as an investment. Now that investment might only be around for three-to-five years. It's much easier for companies to stay flexible by hiring contractors and short-term work. This way they are not tied to the worker, but to the work that needs to be done.

Steven Berkenfeld of Barclays spoke on this very subject:

> When I speak to small companies, emerging companies, the general sense I get is that they will do anything possible not to hire a full-time, permanent employee. There are a lot of real disincentives to hiring people when you can outsource it, and so hiring someone is a big commitment. It comes with a lot of responsibilities and costs for the person doing the hiring throughout the whole tenure of that new employee, and it's something that employers would rather avoid if at all possible.[4]

What we are left with is a workplace that is more individualized and personalized than ever before. Employees will have to brand themselves and show how successful they can be in new environments. Companies will reward employees in unique ways other than monetary rewards. Providing Hack-a-thons, time for inquiry work (like 20% Time), and a bevy of perks are just a few of the ways companies are changing in the 21st century.

Google was not the first company to bring 20% and inquiry time into their everyday work activities. They haven't been the last. In Ryan Tate's book, *The 20% Doctrine,* he demonstrates how tinkering, goofing off, and breaking the rules at work drive success in business. Yes, the exact three things we are constantly yelled at for in school actually help businesses.

In *The 20% Doctrine,* Tate examines how companies large and small can incubate valuable innovative advances by making small, specific changes to how work time is approached within their corporate cultures. The concept of "20% Time" originated at Google, but Tate takes examples from all around the business world—from Yahoo! and Condé Nast to the Thomas Keller Restaurant Group, National Public Radio, Flickr and the *Huffington Post*—to demonstrate how flexibility and experimentation can revolutionize any business model.

We've seen the shift, as Fortune 500 companies have begun embracing strategies used in startups. Those startups like Google, Apple, and Microsoft were all founded by innovators who believe in the power of inquiry. Now those same companies are leading the way for Facebook and every other startup with an idea to change the world. Without inquiry there is little to no innovation. It's our job in education to free up time for innovation. It's our job to open their minds to new ideas. It's our job to prepare them for the present and future possibilities.

What Should a Real Classroom Look Like?

How often do we allow students to "find their talents" in school? Does homework actually prepare students for the real world? And what does the real world look like?

The jobs of the future will fall into three categories: heuristic, evolving, and contracted.

First, jobs will be heuristic. An algorithmic task is one in which you follow a set of established instructions down a single pathway to one conclusion. A heuristic task involves trial and error and discovering the solution by yourself. Algorithmic jobs therefore are ones where the same task is done over and over. Heuristic jobs involve creativity and doing something new often.

Second, jobs will be evolving. If 65 percent of the jobs our children will have don't yet exist, imagine what that number will look like throughout their careers. Positions will evolve, companies will change, and the world will keep innovating. This means our students will have to keep learning with a growth mindset, instead of a fixed view on their job.

Third, jobs will be contracted out. Companies will not want to hire full-time employees, pay for health insurance and waste money on space, when they can contract a great worker to fulfill the task from home. Similarly, individuals will work for themselves, whether that is starting their own micro-business, freelancing, or doing consulting/contracting work.

Sir Ken Robinson has said,

> Public schools were not only created in the interests of industrialism—they were created in the image of industrialism. In many ways, they reflect

> the factory culture they were designed to support. This is especially true in high schools, where school systems base education on the principles of the assembly line and the efficient division of labor.[5]

Students were prepared for algorithmic jobs, because we were living in a very algorithmic society, where the middle class could work at the same company for 30 years and make a decent living. Today, those jobs are disappearing fast. Yet, our classrooms are changing slowly.

Thomas Friedman, author of *The World is Flat,* puts this into some perspective for our educational system:

> In recent years, though, with the leveling of the global playing field, it should be apparent that we are not just competing against ourselves. The opening up of countries like India, China, and Russia means that their young people can plug and play—connect, collaborate, and compete—more easily and cheaply than ever before. And they are. We, alas, are still coasting along as if we have all the time in the world.

Now that we know what the future of work looks like, how can we improve classroom experience so it prepares students for this world?

Classroom Application: Creating Your "Real" Classroom

If we want to model our classrooms on the "real world" we need to change the way we think about instruction and content. The examples below show a distinct connection to skills students will need once they are out of school:

Real World: Work with different people around the globe asynchronously. Need to connect at various times and communicate through writing, phone conversations, and video conferencing.

Real Classroom: Students take part in a "Flat Classroom Project." Your class works with other classes from around the world to research Web 2.0 and Globalization. Students post their video introductions on an online portal. Students share research with group on a wiki or collaborative document. Students then produce a final video explaining their research and the impact it has on the world.

Learn more at http://flatclassroomproject.net/

Real World: Prepared to take on a number of different jobs within a ten-year period. Each job builds on your skill set, and your resume and CV need to keep up with the times.

Real Classroom: Students build digital portfolios that showcase what they have created and made over the years. The portfolio needs to be online and accessible. Their artifacts should be digital and include quotes from classmates, teammates, and teachers. No grades are shared on the portfolio, but instead it is a visual and tangible representation of the kind of work each student produces, both individually and with a team.

Create portfolios using http://sites.google.com/ or http://wordpress.com/

Real World: We learn when we want to. We pick up new ideas and information on the fly (through mobile devices) and at random times.

Real Classroom: The walls of your class must be extended so learning can be extended beyond that 7am–3pm time slot. Setting up a Learning Management System (LMS), or class website is essential. Platforms like Edmodo, Schoology, Moodle, and Blackboard all allow students to access information whenever they want, using a wide variety of devices. Give students the chance to be "on demand" learners.

LMS platforms: http://edmodo.com/; http://schoology.com/; http://coursesites.com/; http://moodle.org/

Real World: Companies and employers are constantly looking at data to improve their performance.

Real Classroom: Use research-based questionnaires from BrightBytes.net or Learning.com to connect your student's assessment scores to related standards and skills for the 21st century. Share the results with colleagues and find ways to improve understanding with their individualized reports.

Real World: We find jobs through having the guts to put ourselves out there for an interview, and the resiliency to keep moving forward even when we face obstacles. We find success through integrity and a tenacity to keep learning and improving.

Real Classroom: Stop grading your students on the same old holistic rubrics. Use the GRIT (Guts, Resiliency, Integrity, and Tenacity) Rubric from College Track to assess students on skills that will prepare them for future success regardless of the job market or position (see the full rubric in Chapter 6).

Learn more about GRIT at http://ajjuliani.com/measuring-the-immeausurable-grit-in-education/

Get out there and innovate in your classroom and in your school. Make it easy. Make it fun. Make it a better experience for our students.

Notes

1 PBS NewsHour, "Should We Fear 'The End of Work'?" by Frank Koller.
2 Will Richardson's "Defining the Problem of Work," http://willrichardson.com/post/55514065443/defining-the-problem-of-work.
3 Anne Fisher, "When Gen X Runs the Show," *Time,* http://content.time.com/time/specials/packages/article/0,28804,1898024_1898023_1898086,00.html.
4 Ibid.
5 www.ted.com/talks/ken_robinson_says_schools_kill_creativity.html.

Reality Check Worksheet

Name: **Date:**

I realize you have big plans for your future. However, the fact is that some people go on to be successful, and others struggle to find a path to success. In the end, success can only be defined by you, and you alone.

Today we are going to do a short "Reality Check" on what you want for your future. Your answers may change over time, but now is the time to start thinking about how you will define success as you move forward in life.

Answer the questions as best you can:

1. What's your name?

2. Who do you want to be?

3. What do you see yourself doing in ten years? What about 20 years?

4. How will you reach that ten-year goal? Write down five steps to get there:

   a.

   b.

   c.

   d.

   e.

5. How will you reach that 20-year goal? Write down five steps to get there:

   a.

   b.

   c.

   d.

   e.

6. What obstacles stand in your way of reaching your goal? Identify three hurdles you must overcome to be successful.

   a.

   b.

   c.

7. Now, let's pull some research. Time to go online. Look up the following information:

   a. What GPA and SAT grades are needed to get into your college of choice?

   b. If you aren't going to college, what skills and certifications are needed for your career of choice?

   c. Who are some successful people in your chosen area? What were their paths to success?

   d. If you are going to be an entrepreneur or start your own business, look up the facts and figures behind new business success.

8. You've done the research. Planned your success. But one thing is missing: You. Doing. It. If some of the results from the reality check put things in perspective that is a good thing. You can never reach the destination unless you know the path.

CHAPTER

2

How 20% Time Changed the World

20% Time may have become famous at Google, but the business idea was originally framed in an education context. This chapter looks at the story of Maria Montessori, her impact on education, and how we can learn from the business sector (just as they learned from us before).

> *Supposing I said there was a planet without schools or teachers, study was unknown, and yet the inhabitants – doing nothing but living and walking about – came to know all things, to carry in their minds the whole of learning: would you not think I was romancing? Well, just this, which seems so fanciful as to be nothing but the invention of a fertile imagination, is a reality. It is the child's way of learning. This is the path he follows. He learns everything without knowing he is learning it, and in doing so passes little from the unconscious to the conscious, treading always in the paths of joy and love.*
>
> *Maria Montessori*[1]

In December of 1913, Maria Montessori came to the United States for a three-week speaking tour. Maria had recently gained fame in international circles for her work with children in Rome, but more specifically for the unorthodox views on early education that drove her instruction. When she arrived in the US she had a worldwide reputation, but was relatively unknown in American education practice. A few months later she left the country famous.

In front of a packed crowd at Carnegie Hall, Maria Montessori spent her time talking to the parents in the audience. Their children, she said, had an untapped potential, one that current schooling procedures did not fully empower. Parents embraced this message and wanted to learn more about methods focusing on the whole child. It was the educators at the hall who were confused. They had heard unconventional theories from an extraordinary woman, but they had no idea how far her ideas on childhood education would spread in the coming century.

Montessori was born in 1870 and became the first female physician in Rome at age 26. Her focus on special needs children led to a study in 1907 where she took 50 poor children from the streets of Rome and educated them in the "Casa dei Bambini." Her adapted curriculum was a surprising success: They learned to read and write at a rapid pace. The children in her class were somewhat of a sight to see, as educators from across the globe came to witness Maria's "school" and rave about the work her children were accomplishing.

The Montessori Method was published in 1909 and translated to English in 1912. It sold over 5,000 copies in the first week and went on to become a bestseller in a matter of months. Montessori's first international training class of teachers began in 1913, but by then there were already hundreds of Montessori schools all over the world. Concerned about many of these schools operating without proper training in her methodology, and unable to contain the international excitement, Montessori was persuaded by publisher Samuel Sidney McClure to visit the US and share her educational vision to teachers, professors, policy makers, and parents.

She was introduced at Carnegie Hall by John Dewey, an American education fixture whose "progressive education" had attracted a large following in the United States. The Montessori Method differed from Dewey's approach, but had also gained prominent followers in the US during this time including Helen Keller, Thomas Edison, Margaret Woodrow Wilson, and Alexander Graham Bell. Mabel Bell, Alexander's wife, had a Montessori class set up for her grandchildren and friends in 1912. By early 1913, she had helped start a private Montessori school in Washington, DC and formed the Montessori Educational Association. She was one of the many people excited to meet Maria in person.

Rita Kramer, author of *Maria Montessori: A Biography,* writes in depth on Maria's tour of the United States, explaining the interest and controversy surrounding her arrival:

> When Maria Montessori arrived in America at the end of 1913 she was at the height of her fame—indeed, one of the most famous women in the world. Newspapers, among them the august *New York Times,* devoted whole pages to interviews with her, and controversy about her ideas raged on the editorial pages and in letters-to-the-editors columns of all the major newspapers. The *New York Tribune* called her the most interesting woman in Europe. The *Brooklyn Daily Eagle* described her as "a woman who revolutionized the educational system of the world . . . the woman who taught the idiot and the insane to read and write—whose success has been so wonderful that the Montessori method has spread into nation after nation as far east as Korea, as far west as Honolulu and south to the Argentine Republic." Even the conservative *New York Sun* noted her arrival in headlines, along with the fact that she brought with her "a new race plan." An eager public was waiting for Montessori in America.[2]

It was Maria's rampant success that led her to the United States, and two years after her talk at Carnegie, she was invited to the Panama–Pacific International

Exposition. At this "World Fair" event in San Francisco she set up a class teaching 21 children with her methods. After four months of observation, the results and reviews were enough to change the minds of many in education.

Then the world changed during World War I. The focus on education was lost in a sea of fighting and rebuilding. Within five years Montessori was all but forgotten by the American public, and a short decade later only a few in education would recognize her name.

Her methods slowly regained traction in the US during the 1960s and 1970s. Maria, who passed away in 1952, was never was able to see the renaissance of her ideas as Montessori schools began to repopulate along the East and West coasts and a new generation found relevance in this way of learning.

Almost 90 years after Maria Montessori's famous speech at Carnegie, Larry Page and Sergey Brin's Silicon Valley startup "Google" went public. Google brought information to our fingertips and re-invented how we "search." Interestingly, the two founders have credited their early Montessori education for their success in starting and running their company.

From Education to Innovation

Sergey Brin's family came to the US when he was six years old and immediately placed him in a Montessori school. Although they were, in his words, "penniless," his parents valued the methods and philosophies of this type of education. Larry Page went to a Montessori school for kindergarten and when the two met at Stanford 12 years later, their shared experience led to each having—as Page would put it—outspoken and obnoxious personalities.

The influence of the Montessori methods spread into their own management philosophies at Google. It was here that 20% Time took on a life of its own. The basic idea behind Google's "20% Time" was to promote innovation and cross-department collaboration between programmers.

This idea was implemented in earlier companies such as 3M, who decided in 1948 that employees should have 15 percent of their time to innovate and work on new product ideas that they may not have had time to follow up on. One of the most famous products to come from this 15% Time is "Post-It Notes." Developed in 1974 by Art Fry, Post-Its have been joined by clear bandages, optical films that reflect light, and painter's tape as products created in 3M's 15% Time.

Google's 20% Time has been similarly successful. It has led to such products as Gmail, Google News, Orkut, Google Sky, Google Talk, and AdSense. Marissa Meyer, Google's former Vice President of Search Products and User Experience (and current Yahoo! CEO), has said that "half of all new product launches had originated" in this 20% Time (see Table 2.1).

Table 2.1 New Products Launched During Google's 20% Time

Date	*Product*
2004	Gmail
2004	AdWords/AdSense
2005	Google Talk
2006	Google News
2006	Orkut
2007	Google Earth
2007	Google Moderator
2007	Google.org

While this time has ultimately led to great products, it is important to note how this policy reflects Google's company culture of innovation and experimentation. Creative and self-directed people want to work at Google, and it shows: *Forbes* magazine ranked Google as its top company to work for in the 2012 listing of the "100 Best Companies to Work For." Google speaks about their ideal culture by saying the following:

> Our founders built Google around the idea that work should be challenging, and the challenge should be fun. We believe that great, creative things are more likely to happen with the right company culture—and that doesn't just mean lava lamps and rubber balls. There is an emphasis on team achievements and pride in individual accomplishments that contribute to our overall success. We put great stock in our employees—energetic, passionate people from diverse backgrounds with creative approaches to work, play and life. Our atmosphere may be casual, but as new ideas emerge in a café line, at a team meeting or at the gym, they are traded, tested and put into practice with dizzying speed—and they may be the launch pad for a new project destined for worldwide use.[3]

Google's culture and 20% Time ties into the very same beliefs of the Montessori Method. Maria's focus was not merely on education, but on learning. While Montessori schools can still be found throughout the world it is her ideas on learning that have spread farther than Google. For example:

- Individualized learning based on interests
- Hands-on learning opportunities
- Freedom to explore
- Don't interrupt a work cycle or "flow"
- Work at your own pace

- Focus on the whole child
- Teaching instead of correcting

Despite the lauded success of these ideas in the business world, much of our current K-12 learning environment gives no time for students to choose their own learning topics and materials. This book sets out to help educators bring these timely and all-important ideas into every classroom, by giving a clear framework for success that can be tied to any set of standards.

The Real Issue with Our Educational System

The world has changed since Maria Montessori came to the US with her controversial ideas. We are able to connect quicker, collaborate easier, and learn about anything we desire. In fact, the 21st-century workforce is all about learning. Futurist Alvin Toffler explains this new reality succinctly: "In the future illiteracy will not be defined by those who cannot read and write, but by those who cannot learn and relearn."[4]

We are no longer educating students to get a job they can keep for 30 years and retire. We are not educating them to be in the same profession where their skill set does not change. We are not educating them to find stability or comfort.

Instead, we are educating our students for a job which most likely does not yet exist. For a world we cannot foresee, and for a workforce that has doubled in the past ten years thanks to technology and globalization.

So I ask: Is our current system educating students to be innovative, creative, and adaptable?

In his book, *That Used To Be Us* (2011), Thomas Friedman emphasizes two developments that have changed the world forever: globalization and the information technology (IT) revolution.

Globalization impacts every one of us right now. Globalization has led to offshoring, outsourcing, and a large number of newly educated individuals. Friedman references how much of an impact globalization has:

> Globalization has pulled millions of people out of poverty in India and China, and multiplied the size of the global middle class. It has raised the global standard of living faster than that at any other time in the history of the world, and it is supporting astounding growth. All world economic activity was valued at $7 trillion in 1950. That's equal to how much growth took place over just the past decade, even including the recent downturn.[5]

It is globalization that has "flattened our world" and education has leveled the playing field for students and workers around the world to compete for jobs better than ever before. Companies in this globalized world—like Google, Yahoo!, and 3M—are only successful when they innovate, and they need innovative policies and employees for that to happen.

The IT revolution is similarly providing new solutions for jobs that used to be handled by people. Remember calling to schedule a flight, book reservations at a hotel, and rent a car? Now you can do all three of those things in less than ten minutes on a computer without ever talking to a person.

There are still manufacturing jobs to be had, but the ones that aren't being outsourced need highly qualified workers. On November 11, 2012, *60 Minutes* reported that manufacturers in America are looking for over 3,000,000 new employees. However, they need properly trained, skilled, and motivated workers. Long gone are the days where you could show up, work mindlessly for eight hours, and clock out. Companies today are looking for programmers that can operate complex machinery, make quick and strong decisions, and be adaptable to changing conditions.

Many are calling for a complete overhaul of the education system in the US and in other countries around the world. Some, like Sir Ken Robinson, believe we are "killing the creativity" in our schools.[6] Yet, it is difficult to change an entire system, and teachers have to work within their school parameters for the time being.

The questions are therefore: Where does that leave us with our current education system? And what can we do within the confines of our current curriculum and national mandates?

The 20% Solution

Montessori's methods have prevailed through globalization and the IT revolution because they promote intellectual curiosity and creativity. Google took it a step further when they mandated 20% Time. It forced their employees to start with something they were interested in and try to grow it exponentially. This push for innovation and creativity led to an intrinsic desire to improve and build upon past successes. Montessori and Google have not only influenced education and business with this approach, but also have changed the world with their ideas and products.

In the classroom, 20% Time is a simple change with huge implications. When I gave my students 20% Time to explore their passions and learn what they were interested in, it opened the door for valuable learning experiences and conversations I never could have expected.

One particular student had always been interested in writing her own original songs. She had written over 20 songs but never recorded or performed a song for anyone other than herself. She came to me asking if it was "ok" to go into more depth about the recording process. Of course I said, "Yes!" After reading, researching, and talking to other experts about recording she set out to release her music to the world. Her final product was two recorded songs and a "how-to" guide for other students looking to create and produce their own music. Our class learned so much about her that we did not know before, and were able to help spread her music by sharing it online.

If you want to prepare students for life after school, 20% Time and inquiry-driven learning is a must. Students don't need to fill in answer sheets or bubbles on a piece of paper. They need to be given the time to produce something of value, to themselves and the world. In 20% Time projects they have to demonstrate that they can do the following:

1. Brainstorm and come up with a way to explore their passions, while creating a final product.
2. Research and comb through a litany of resources on their topic.
3. Write reflections and informational pieces on what they have learned.
4. Share and collaborate with fellow students on their ideas.
5. Reach out to experts around the world about their idea and learn from the best.
6. Create a product that demonstrates a true understanding of their work.
7. Reflect on their work and that of their classmates.
8. Share their ideas and products with the world.

The blueprint for success is not in the blueprint itself, but instead in what it represents; 20% Time can be done in a variety of shapes and forms. This book allows you to give your students the freedom to explore, create, and possibly change the world.

Classroom Application: Sample 20% Time Projects that Foster Innovative Thinking

Sign-Language Project

What: Learn and perform song in sign-language.

Why: To be able to communicate with my cousin who is deaf and have fun.

How: Study sign-language book, watch videos, practice with myself in front of mirror, and talk to others that sign.

Making Science Accessible

What: Clone a carnivorous plant in my own kitchen.

Why: Science is usually portrayed as some difficult thing to do in a lab. You can "do science" anywhere using household items.

How: Using basic items I can get at Wal-Mart, I'll create a clone of a carnivorous plant in my kitchen.

Creating Anti-Bullying Campaign

What: Create a Facebook group—Wiss Compliments—that focuses on sharing positives about random people in our school.

Why: Too much emphasis on "bullying" is focused on what one person does wrong. Let's change that to focus on giving tons of compliments to outweigh those bullies.

How: Start the group anonymously and share it on Facebook with students in the school and start complimenting. Start the movement and watch it grow.

Making a Video Game for Younger Students on Digital Citizenship

What: Create a video game that teachers younger students about digital citizenship and our digital footprint.

Why: It's one thing when a teacher or parent tells a younger student about digital citizenship, but we feel a video game can be a more effective tool for them to understand the consequences of online behavior.

Notes

1 *Maria Montessori: A Biography,* Rita Kramer (www.ritakramer.com/maria_montessori__a_biography_31080.htm).
2 Ibid.
3 Google's Company Philosophy (www.google.com/about/company/philosophy/).
4 From AlvinToffler.com and *Wired* magazine.
5 Newsweek 2010 Review, "Overblown Fears," Thomas Friedman (http://2010.newsweek.com/top-10/most-overblown-fears/globalization.html).
6 www.ted.com/talks/ken_robinson_says_schools_kill_creativity.html

Interview Questions from Big Companies

When we think about getting a job at Apple, Google, or Amazon we usually think about the steps leading up to that job, and what qualifications we need. Rarely do we ever ask ourselves, "What kinds of questions will these companies ask in an interview?"

A great activity to do with students is to ask these questions as writing prompts to start the class and get their innovative minds thinking. When they find out the questions are from a Google interview, they'll usually be excited to answer!

Amazon asks: "Jeff Bezos walks into your office and says you can have a million dollars to launch your best entrepreneurial idea. What is it?"

Dell asks: "What songs best describe your work ethic?"

Apple asks: "What kind of animal would you be and why?"

Jiffy Software asks: "Have you ever stolen a pen from work?"

Google asks: "How many cows are in Canada?"

Kimberly-Clark asks: "If you had turned your cell phone to silent, and it rang really loudly despite it being on silent, what would you tell me?"

LivingSocial asks: "What's your favorite song? Perform it for us now."

Zappos asked: "What superhero would you be and would you dress up at work given the chance?"

Gallop asked: "What do you think about when you are alone in your car?"

JetBlue asked: "How many quarters would you need to reach the height of the Empire State building?"

Clark Construction Group asked candidates for an engineer position: "A penguin walks through that door right now wearing a sombrero. What does he say and why is he here?"

PricewaterhouseCoopers asked: “My wife and I are going on vacation, where would you recommend?”

Bain & Company asked: “Estimate how many windows are in New York.”

Read more: http://www.businessinsider.com/weird-interview-questions-from-apple-google-amazon-2013-9?op=1#!JsL3s

CHAPTER

3

History Repeats Itself . . . In a Good Way

Innovation has always been a part of human history. Some of the greatest innovators of our times were not very good students, but instead used an inquiring mind to spark their success. This chapter provides a historical perspective on innovation, and a framework for bringing it back into our classrooms.

There is a famous saying from Albert Einstein that many teachers like to quote: "Everyone is a genius. But if you judge a fish by its ability to climb a tree, it will live its whole life believing that it is stupid."

Most often I see this quote associated with the high-stakes testing movement, and other forms of education reform. I actually used to nod my head when I read this quote, silently saying, "Yep, that's right. You can't force a student to be something they aren't." Shame on me.

Agreeing with this quote is giving in to the notion that kids have limitations they can't overcome. And that's not right. Instead, my motto I spent the past few years focusing on is "teaching fish how to climb trees." Crazy? I don't think so.

The mudskipper fish is rarely talked about. There aren't competitions on TV to catch mudskippers, and I have yet to see a picture of someone holding up the fresh mudskipper they just caught on a big fishing trip. However, the mudskippers are probably the best "land-adapted" of contemporary fish. They are able to spend days moving about out of water and can even climb mangroves.

Yep, that's right. The ol' mudskipper fish can climb a tree. I'm sure all its fish friends and teachers probably told him it was "impossible" or that he'd be "stupid" to try it. But he went with it anyway, and eventually joined the ranks of flying and jumping fish as geniuses.

As a teacher, I realized that my students may come into class with varying levels of skills and talents. I see the same thing as a coach. But it would be foolish for me to pigeon-hole any of my students or players into a "role" or "category." Usually, it's those students who overcome obstacles and the "impossible" that end up being remarkable. And that's what I want all of our students and players to be: remarkable.

Here are just a few examples of students "climbing trees":

Nick D'Aloisio started his company "Summly" at age 15. At age 17 he sold it to Yahoo! for $30 million. Nick said in a Business Insider interview: "When I founded Summly at 15, I would have never imagined being in this position so suddenly. I'd personally like to thank Li Ka-Shing and Horizons Ventures for having the foresight to back a teenager pursuing his dream. Without you all, this never would have been possible. I'd also like to thank my family, friends and school for supporting me."

Katie Davis left over Christmas break of her senior year for a short mission trip to Uganda and her life was turned completely upside down. She was so uniquely affected by the people of Uganda and the needs of their children, Katie planned to return and care for them. Katie has adopted 13 Ugandan children and has established a ministry, Amazima, that feeds and sends hundreds more to school. You can read about her story in *Kisses From Katie*.

When 12-year-old Steven Gonzalez Jr. was diagnosed with Acute Myelogenous Leukemia, a rare form of cancer, doctors said that he had a 2 percent chance to live. But he beat the odds and survived, though his weak immune system forced him into isolation for 100 days. He credits video games for helping him through the rough experience. Gonzalez wanted to help other cancer patients his age, and so he created a video game, "Play Against Cancer," in which players destroy cancer cells illustrated as green ghosts. He also developed "The Survivor Games," a social network and online community for teen cancer patients.[1]

Five-year-old Phoebe Russell needed to complete a community service project before she could graduate from kindergarten. Uninterested in a lemonade stand, she saw a homeless man begging for food and decided to raise $1,000 for the San Francisco Food Bank. Her teacher tried to lower expectations to something more reasonable, but Phoebe's heartwarming appeal to leave soda cans and donations at the school snowballed. Before she knew it, Phoebe had raised $3,736.30– the equivalent of 17,800 heated meals.[2]

These are just a few of the thousands of stories out there of kids doing the impossible. I'm sure there are many stories of teachers doing the impossible. When we look at innovation in the classroom, and in the real world, it is not connected solely to technology. The innovation always has a purpose that resonates with the innovator, and it's rarely (if ever) forced. People fail to innovate when you tell them what to do. This is the same for students. No one forces true innovation, especially a teacher in a classroom.

No One Forces True Innovation

Thomas Edison was a poor kid. The type of kid that teachers sometimes sadly write off. Then one of his teachers called him "addled" (unable to think clearly), and his mother took him out of school. It was the best thing for him. She taught him basic reading, writing, and math concepts; but, the majority of Edison's schooling came from his own reading, and his constant tinkering with mechanical and chemical experiments. When Edison left home to be on his own at age 16, it was with all the confidence in the world. He later said, "My mother was the making of me. She was so true, so sure of me, and I felt I had someone to live for, someone I must not disappoint."

The greatest inventor of modern times went on to create the phonograph, a working electric and lightbulb system, and the first forms of the "motion picture," which he dubbed a "Kinetoscope." Edison failed early, and he failed often. One of his biggest failures was trying to mine iron ore. He ended up selling all of his stock in General Electric to fund this project that never succeeded. What we remember him for is his 1,093 patents, and his innovative spirit that impacted our world today.

Grace Murray Hopper joined the Navy in 1943 and was stationed at Harvard University. It was at Harvard where Hopper began work on IBM's Harvard Mark I computer. Admiral Hopper's work at Harvard led her to invent the "compiler": Its basic function was to translate English commands into computer code. Programmers could now create code quicker and easier than ever before. Her second compiler was named the "Flow-Matic." It was used to program UNIVAC I and II (the first commercially available computers in the USA). Admiral Hopper faced many challenges in her time innovating, and failed often. Her final invention was a collaborative effort, as she oversaw the development of COBOL, one of the earliest computer programming languages that paved the way for the programmers of today.

Steve Wozniak, one of the most famous programmers and innovators of our time, created the Apple I and II personal computer. No one told Steve Wozniak to make the Apple computer. He had a great job with Hewlett-Packard working on scientific calculators. But Steve had been building computers and other electronics since high school. His main goal was to build a computer that was cheap, easy to program, and simple for the end user. The Apple I covered the first two points, but the Apple II made "simplicity" its main goal.

Wozniak didn't have a fancy office, lab, or resources. Instead, he built these computers on the cheap. Teaming up with Steve Jobs they were able to create, market, and change the entire computer industry. Wozniak never stopped tinkering, improving, and making.

Why Does Innovative History Repeat Itself?

What can we learn from history's greatest innovators? No one is going to "make" the next great invention because they were told to do so. Innovation most often comes from personal inquiry. Steven Johnson is the author of *Where Good Ideas*

Come From. In his book, Johnson argues there are seven patterns of innovation that are repeated in nature and culture. Johnson's seven patterns are:

1. The Adjacent Possible: New ideas are rarely all that new. Innovation comes from building on previous ideas and connecting our ideas to as many people and places as possible.
2. Liquid Networks: The elements of an idea are worthless unless they are properly connected. Liquid networks allow for those connections, and collisions, to happen between all ideas.
3. The Slow Hunch: It usually takes time for ideas to connect and evolve into something tangible. The hunch allows people's ideas to grow and morph. This is why a "commonplace book" is so important. Collect all of your ideas and small bits of information. Then let them grow.
4. Serendipity: Innovation is rarely planned. However, one key condition is that the discovery must be meaningful to "you." There has to be a purpose and reason, or a hunch will never materialize into a connection.
5. Error: Noise and error are often associated with unpredictability. Unpredictability is a key component to innovation. Fail fast and keep moving on. Innovation will then happen.
6. Exaptation: Allow for diversification in ideas and connections. This way a combination of ideas can connect to accidentally tackle new problems.
7. Platforms: Google is the best example of a platform for innovation. The company's procedures encourage collaboration, the sharing of new and old ideas, and experimentation. A platform is a place where the other innovative patterns exist in community.

It is through these patterns that we can envision what would make a truly innovative learning experience. Too often our classrooms fail to give students an opportunity to innovate. Instead we tend to focus on assessing comprehension and understanding through fixed tasks. Johnson makes it clear: *Ideas need to be free to spark innovation*.

Building a Community of Innovators

In 1995 Paul Graham co-founded Viaweb, the first software-as-a-service (saas) company. Yahoo! acquired Viaweb in 1998 where it ultimately became Yahoo! Store. Graham is now somewhat of a legend in Silicon Valley, but not for his success with Viaweb. In 2005 Graham co-founded the "Y Combinator" with Jessica Livingston, Robert Morris, and Trevor Blackwell. This new type of startup incubator has gone on to fund over 450 startups, including Dropbox, Airbnb, Stripe, and Reddit. In fact, the average value of a Y Combinator financed company is $22.4 million.

The premise of Y Combinator (YC) was simple. Graham and Livingston believed startup funding was backwards. Graham told Livingston on a walk home from dinner, "investors should be making more, smaller investments, they should be funding hackers instead of suits, and they should be willing to fund younger founders." They planned on giving a small investment (around $10 000) to a batch of startups, and in return they would own 10 percent of each company, and help it find success.

Now, Y Combinator runs two three-month funding cycles a year, one from January through March and one from June through August. Graham explains on the Y Combinator site:

> We ask the founders of each startup to move to the Bay Area for the duration of their cycle, during which our team works with them to get the company into the best shape possible. Each cycle culminates in an event called Demo Day, at which the startups present to an audience that now includes most of the world's top startup investors.

Y Combinator is the most successful incubator of its kind. But this was not by accident. The founders set up a platform where specific patterns of innovation could happen at any time. Let's look at how YC functions as a community of innovators.

Team Dinners

During each funding cycle, YC hosts a weekly dinner for all of the new startups. This dinner is a time for conversation, sharing of ideas, and a chance to listen to a successful startup founder. All of the teams congregate in a large hall and informally share what they are working on. The speaker (someone like Mark Zuckerberg) arrives before dinner and gets to talk with teams before giving a talk over dessert. The talks are never recorded or released to the public in any way. This allows for a more candid story from the founder, and details that may have not yet been heard. After a Q&A session, they break up into informal groups again, speaking late into the night.

These dinners provide the perfect platform for Johnson's patterns of "the adjacent possible" and "liquid networks." The informality of the presentation gives another level of exaptation, as a diverse group of speakers share throughout the three-month cycle.

Office Hours

Remember having office hours with professors in college? I rarely attended these sessions unless I was in dire need of an extension, or review. Office hours at the Y Combinator are a bit different. The startups need to book the appointments, but there is no limit to how much time they can book. The conversations revolve around ideas, problems, and potential solutions. The advisors are all successful founders willing to give advice, but also listen.

Office hours provide a nice platform for the "slow hunch" to materialize. Often companies at YC have a great idea that needs tweaking or changing. The purpose during office hours is for each startup to have a strong sense of what Johnson calls "serendipity." It also allows for teams to share their failures, and learn from previous errors in the process.

Alumni Connections

Now that YC has been around for seven years, and has funded more than 450 startups, the alumni network is large and influential. Paul Graham consistently invites alumni back to take part in events, hear company demos before they talk to investors, and share their stories at the team dinners. However, it is the informal connections that really prove to be of value. This network is open and willing to help share ideas. They provide the larger continuing platform once the three-month cycle has ended. Founders of many YC companies have gone on to start a second or third startup, with much help from this Alumni Network.

A Y Combinator is an interesting term in computer science. It is basically a "program that runs programs." The Y Combinator that Paul Graham runs is a "business that funds businesses." In each case, the platform is built for success because it can grow and expand. That is what we want with education: To give our students the chance to grow and expand as learners.

Classroom Application: A Framework for Innovation in Education

Innovation can be difficult to foster in some school settings. However, we have a responsibility to prepare our students for a future which requires creative and innovative thinkers. Instead of focusing on how to force students to innovate, I argue we should allow for Johnson's patterns to naturally create ideas and connections. In order to do this, we must set up the learning experience as a platform.

Allow For . . .

Collaboration

Students must have opportunities to collaborate, and just as we saw with Y Combinator, it should be collaboration with peers and mentors. Cross-discipline collaboration is necessary for ideas to evolve and connect. Global collaboration among peers in projects like "The Flat Classroom Project" and "Quad-blogging" also allow for the adjacent possible to take place.

Failure

Do you give your students tests? Do you then allow students to learn from their failures on the test and re-take it? Furthermore, we should allow students to fail in a variety of ways: formal and informal assessments, written pieces, projects, and discussions. With failure comes growth. Allow for failure and your students will see it as part of the learning process, not the end of the learning process.

Inquiry

Innovation usually starts with a question. There is a great Chinese proverb that says, "He who asks a question is a fool for five minutes; he who does not ask a question remains a fool forever." Inquiry in our classrooms is an opportunity for everyone to learn, not just the student with the question. Stop focusing on getting the "right answer" and start focusing on more questions.

Make Time For . . .

Reflection

Confucius said, "By three methods we may learn wisdom: First, by reflection, which is noblest; second, by imitation, which is easiest; and third by experience, which is the bitterest." Making time for reflection in the classroom is akin to making time for eating after cooking. Students have to be able to think about their learning process, and how they could have improved, what they could have done differently. Without reflection, we lose the ability to learn from error and have slow hunches grow.

Sharing

Let's face it: The *Think, Pair, Share* instructional strategy is not real sharing. Despite what you've been told in school, making students think on their own for 2 minutes, then pair up with another student to share what they thought about for a minute, does not meet the quota for sharing in a classroom! However, we can learn from the model of *Think, Pair, Share*. Students need to be given opportunity to share before the creative process, during the creative process, and after during reflection. Sharing should be open and not given a time limit; it is one of the most powerful forces of innovation.

Tinkering

We give children time to play and tinker all the time. It's actually not until they go to school that our children lose the time to make scenes out of Legos, cardboard people, and countless figures glued and taped together. As we saw with Montessori's educational practices, students can make amazing and useful creations when given the opportunity.

Support . . .

New Ideas

If you allow for collaboration, failure, and inquiry in the classroom, and make time for reflection, sharing, and tinkering . . . then new ideas will emerge. At this junction, the role of a teacher, and the class, must be to support this new idea. Many times we are quick to judge a new idea, or attack its merit with conventional wisdom. An innovative classroom questions new ideas, and also connects them to adjacent possibilities.

Project-Based Learning

Research has shown that project-based learning has documented improvements such as increases in the ability to define problems, reason with clear arguments, and plan projects. Edutopia reports that, "Additional research has documented improvements in motivation, attitude toward learning, and work habits. Students who struggle in traditional instructional settings have often excelled when working on a project, which better matches their learning style or preference for collaboration." Projects can serve as the platform for the other patterns of innovation to co-exist and connect.

On Demand Learning

My daughter is four years old. She doesn't have to wait for much. If she wants to watch *Doc McStuffins* she can get six different show options on demand. Or she can play a game or access those same shows from an iPad. If my wife and I aren't around to read to her, she can open up an eBook that reads to her as she turns the pages. That same iPad (or any other tablet) can let her practice ABCs, work on her numbers, or just give her a space to paint and be artsy.

She is growing up and living in the "On Demand" generation. It's a generation that has constant access to what we used to wait for. We can't limit the educational experience to inside the classroom walls. We must provide learning resources, and collaborative abilities, for students to access at any time. This is why Learning Management Systems like Edmodo, Schoology, Moodle, and Blackboard are so important. They extend learning to be an "anytime, anywhere" experience. Make sure your students have this freedom.

Assess . . .

Growth

Carol Dweck, the author of *Mindset: The New Psychology of Success,* speaks about growth: "IF, like those with the growth mindset, you believe you can develop yourself, then you're open to accurate information about your current abilities, even if it's unflattering. What's more, if you're oriented toward learning, as they are, you need accurate information about your current abilities in order to learn effectively." Let's forget about assessing the "finished product," and instead worry about our students continually growing. This is differentiation at its finest: Students build on their own learning and on learning from others. Their paces may be different, but they all have the ability to create something amazing.

Critical Thinking

Critical thinking is often a term thrown into lesson plans and rubrics without much thought behind it. Sure, we want to see our students "thinking outside the box" but what does that really mean? And more importantly, what does it look like?

Critical thinking is when students solve a problem with their own knowledge. This can happen individually or in groups. Inquiry will lead students to a long list of problems and issues that they will have to solve. By allowing students to find the answers themselves, and create new solutions, we can see critical thinking in action.

GRIT

Professor Angela Lee Duckworth, a research psychologist at the University of Pennsylvania, examines two traits that predict success: grit, the tendency to sustain interest and effort in pursuing long-term goals, and self-control, the regulation of behavioral, emotional, and attentional impulses. Grit is an oft-used term in education reform circles, but it is hard to assess in our students.

As mentioned in Chapter 1, the College Track program in San Francisco has eased some of that difficulty by creating a "GRIT Rubric" for their after-school preparatory program. College Track has broken the word Grit down to four factors: Guts, Resilience, Integrity, and Tenacity.

Make History Repeat Itself

The stories of Thomas Edison, Admiral Hopper, and Steve Wozniak are not anomalies. There are students doing innovative work in classrooms around the world right now. However, we tend to view these students and their accomplishments as unique. Instead, our focus has to be on making school a place where innovation happens all the time. As we prepare students for the future of work, it is essential for innovative patterns to be present in our educational system.

Notes

1 "Kids Code the Darndest Things" on Mashable.
2 "10 Great Philanthropists Who Are Kids" on Listverse.

Ways to Get Students Coding and Making

We learned in this chapter that many of the great inventors and innovators of our time got their start early on in life. That's why it is so important to get our students coding and making at the elementary and middle school levels. Use these five quick tips to get students making and coding in your classroom.

Start Small

Give students a small project to work with a program they already know. Students can "build" in *Minecraft, SimCity* (and other Sims), *Google SketchUp,* or other games they already use on a regular basis. The thought is that we can change the mindset of students to "consume" with these games and programs, and instead start to "create."

Make Digital into Physical, or Physical into Digital

An easy strategy to start with is to take digital products and make them into physical products. Make a "real life" *Minecraft* or video game setting. Take a favorite outfit of one of your TV show characters and make it for yourself. Take a picture from online and turn it into a physical product. The opposite way is to take a physical product and create it digitally. Depending on your computer availability you can switch the parameters of the project.

Use Student-Friendly Programming Apps

You can use a variety of tools and programs to enable students to actually start coding, but my three favorite for younger students are Scratch, Lego Mindstorms, and Simple.

- Scratch was developed by MIT Labs that over 800,000 people (kids mostly) have used to make in the region of 1.7 million projects. Projects are easy to create, and students can make anything from games to animations.
- Lego Mindstorms allows your students to build robots! The kits come with easy Lego languages, and students can build and program!
- Simple is a programming language for kids on Windows computers where they can make games, code secret messages, and share their creations with each other. Learn more at www.simplecodeworks.com/.

Give Their "Making" a Purpose

It's always fun to make a game. But it's so much better when students make and create for a purpose. Whether that is a class purpose, community purpose, or individual purpose it's up to you and your class to decide what their efforts should be geared towards.

Reach Out to Experts in the Field as Mentors

Go to Code.org and find a mentor for your class. Reach out to people that will inspire your students to make great things. They'll love you as a teacher for making these connections happen.

CHAPTER

Designing 20% Time for the Classroom

There are a wide variety of obstacles that can hold teachers back from using inquiry-based learning in the classroom. Current curriculum, common core standards, administrative pressures, and parent questions are all difficult to deal with when implementing this type of learning. This chapter provides an overarching view on how to design 20% learning experiences and how to overcome those obstacles through research and best practices.

There is a movement happening in education right now. Maybe you've heard about it, maybe you haven't yet. It comes in various shapes and forms but the end result is the same: Students learning what they want to learn.

Yes, I said it, so let me repeat: Students are learning what they want in classrooms around the world.

What is truly astounding is how interconnected this movement is with the social web. It also is happening at the same time that inquiry-driven professional development movements, such as Edcamp, are catching serious momentum. However, the main difference is that Edcamp can be done on the learner's "own time" while the 20% Time takes place in school with all the stakeholders watching.

Right now (depending on who you are) there are three possible ways to deal with this type of news:

1. **That's awesome.** It is about time that inquiry-driven learning became a reality in school. I want my class/child/school to have that opportunity!
2. **That sounds great, but . . .** I don't think it could really work. How does it tie to curriculum? What about the Common Core? What will parents say? What will my principal say? How can I hold them accountable for learning something?
3. **That's crazy.** Something like that could never work. Once again we are lowering the bar for kids.

I've heard all three viewpoints after writing my first"20% Time (like Google) In My Class" blog post in January of 2012. I've learned so much more about inquiry-driven personal learning time since that post and have been able to connect with amazing educators who are doing similar projects in their classes: Kevin Brookhouser, Juan De Luca, Joy Kirr, Denise Krebs, Gallit Zvi, Hugh McDonald, Dr. Jackie Gerstein, and Angela Maiers, or in their schools: Chris Lehmann, Matt Bebbington, and Josh Stumpenhorst (to name just a few).

This chapter is meant to address the three points-of-view above. The research, stories from other educators, and my own experiences over the past year will have you ready to start your own 20% project.

The "This is Awesome" Group

It's important to have a real purpose behind this project. My purpose was to enable my 11th grade students to start taking control of their own learning. They've been told what to do (for the most part) in school and in their own life for the better part of 16 years. This project allowed them to make all the choices and have OWNERSHIP in their learning. Kevin Brookhouser has a well-crafted letter he sent home with his students that you can check out on his blog: www.iteachithink.com/2012/08/a-letter-to-my-students-and-parents.html.

The Genius Hour guidelines also set the tone for the project. Make sure you are comfortable with the set-up of your project before handing it out to students. There will be a lot of questions . . . blank stares . . . and happy faces. Be ready to handle each type of student.

A fantastic rubric was put together by Denise Krebs, and displays Genius Hour guidelines in a way that is easy for students, parents, and other colleagues to understand (see Table 4.1).

My project had five main components that helped it run successfully. While other variables may change, these are my recommendations based on my experience.

Structure Unstructured Time

Students need to have their "20% Time" structured in a way that makes sense with your schedule. For elementary classrooms that may be every day before lunch/recess and for secondary students it may be on Fridays, or a specific time during the week, etc. If you give them their 20% at random times without being able to prepare it may hurt the effectiveness in the short- and long-term. This may even mean a discussion with students at the start of the project of what time would work best.

Don't Grade the Final Product

Hey, I understand the need for grades. They help us dictate to the students what they are mastering and what they need to work on; they help motivate

Table 4.1 Genius Hour Rubric Genius = Creating and producing. That's from the original meaning of the word.

Quality	*Yes, I have it! (5)*	*Where are you on the continuum between "Yes, I have it!" (5) and "Not yet!" (1)*	*Not yet! (1)*
Ambiguity. I'm OK with a little confusion, knowing there is more than one way to do the job.	I don't need to ask the teacher a lot of questions. I can think for myself and get the job done.	5 4 3 2 1	I have to be told exactly how to do every job. There is only one right way to do the job.
Inquisitiveness. I ask questions and want answers.	I am curious and I look up things that interest me. I'm a lifelong learner.	5 4 3 2 1	I don't ask questions just for the joy of learning, and I don't really want to learn new things.
Generating Ideas (brainstorming). I create lots of possible ideas.	I am able to fluently create a list of ideas. I use my imagination.	5 4 3 2 1	I cannot see beyond the obvious ideas. I am easily frustrated. I may be lazy.
Originality of Ideas. I create unique ideas!	I can think outside the box and I have a great imagination. I think of ideas that others never even thought of.	5 4 3 2 1	I can only think of ideas that others thought of first. I don't like new ways of doing things. I just want to stick with the old way.
Flexibility/ Adaptability. Mentally, I can bend easily any which way and not break.	I can think of new ways to do things when I get stuck. I can recognize other people's good ideas.	5 4 3 2 1	I am not willing to change my ideas or think of better ones.
Self-Reflection. I can look honestly at myself and evaluate my work.	I can honestly go through my work and know what's right or wrong.	5 4 3 2 1	I lie about my work. I can't or won't look honestly at the things I do well and the things that need more work.
Intrinsic Motivation. I want to do it. I know the purpose and it pleases me.	I want to try new things. I believe in myself.	5 4 3 2 1	Not willing to try new things unless I get something for it. Sometimes I say, "I don't care," even about Genius Hour.

(*Continued*)

Table 4.1 (*Continued*)

Quality	*Yes, I have it! (5)*	*Where are you on the continuum between "Yes, I have it!" (5) and "Not yet!" (1)*	*Not yet! (1)*
Risk Taking. I'm not afraid to try something difficult for fear of failure. As Edison said: "I have not failed . . . I have succeeded in proving that 1000 ways will not work."	I'm not afraid to try anything even if I don't do well at it. I keep trying and find a new way that might work.	5 4 3 2 1	I don't try new things for fear of failing. I try a couple of times and then give up altogether.
Expertise. I am proud and thankful to know a lot about one or more subjects. I am an expert.	I know I am good at one or more things, and I am not afraid to share my knowledge with others.	5 4 3 2 1	I don't try to be expert at anything. I don't want to be. Or I pretend to not know anything.
Persistence. I can stick with a project even when it gets hard. I understand that the word "passion" comes from the base word for "suffering."	When the going gets tough, I work harder. I have grit, determination, and perseverance. I want to keep going and finish a difficult task.	5 4 3 2 1	I usually quit when I run into a snag. I switch Genius Hour projects often whenever it gets too hard.

Getting ready for Genius Hour . . . What question do you want to answer? What do you need to do to get ready? How can your teacher help you get ready?

Courtesy of Denise Krebs

many students; and they provide a measure for parents and other stakeholders in the educational process to view academic achievement. However, in terms of personal learning time, there should not be a grade for the finished product. This should be inquiry-driven, intrinsically motivated learning. Students can be assessed on their effort, but I would not do that with grades at the end of a project. This is when teacher conferencing (during the 20% Time) becomes important and useful in order to touch base and help students move forward. Sometimes grading diminishes the intellectual curiosity from the project, and allows for external motivations. In terms of external motivations, I believe there should only be one allowed (see next section). If you want to see how I handled students who might not work as hard without a grade, read the next section. *This is an area that has been debated and changed by other 20% teachers. It worked well with 11th graders, but might not work with ninth graders, middle school, or elementary students.*

Peer Accountability

Peer pressure is one of the best, and worst, types of external motivation. We tend to look at peer pressure as a negative external force that causes students to do things they normally wouldn't do. Consequently, we sometimes forget that the flip side of peer pressure is "peer accountability": Students doing well and working hard because their peers are working hard and doing well. Ray Fisman wrote a great article in 2010 about "The Right Kind of Peer Pressure" in schools (particularly with girls) based on studies by Cornell researchers.[1]

In terms of personalized learning time, you need to facilitate a collaborative learning space where students can see what other students are doing in real-time. Having students post projects up on the web is also another great idea because they'll see what their peers are doing with their time. While the project itself allows for students to be individuals, sometimes seeing a friend moving forward will give a needed boost to others in the class.

Reflection

I had the meta-cognitive part of the project be student journals. While these were not graded, I did routinely check what they were writing about the project and their own personal learning. Some students wanted guiding questions and I helped them, but did not require answers to those questions. I learned from their reflections, and doing them meant that they could look back on what they had learned throughout the project.

Presentation (Sharing)

Periodically I had students share their journals (or a line or two about their project) on our class's LMS (learning management system)—which was Schoology. Students could then comment on what they thought about each other's work, and give each other "likes." This connects back to "No Grade" because I was assessing them through their work here without grades, and connects to the "Peer Accountability" and "Reflection" components as well with student feedback.

They also presented to the entire class at the end of the third and fourth marking periods. This was an informal presentation, but I had each student stand in front of the class and speak about what they did. Other teachers have done TED style presentations, and you can decide what will work best for your grade level. Some students spoke longer and brought in props or slides, while others talked about what they did as if they were telling a story. It was obvious which students were proud of what they did, and which ones wished they'd spent some more time/energy on their project. I think it would have been even better if this was started in the beginning of the year with four presentations throughout.

Finally, I'd recommend that students have some type of "product" at the end of their 20% Time. This is something I did not stress during my first project, but now that I've helped start three other projects at my school, it is a big help to the students in framing "what" they are going to do.

Implementation Options

1. Collaboration. (Are you going to allow students to work in groups if they have similar interests and/or passions?)
2. Technology. (Is this a requirement? Can students bring in their own computers to class if need be? Think about your technological needs.)
3. Standards and the Common Core. (Being an English teacher I was able to connect many of our state standards to the project.)
4. Parental involvement. (I didn't send a letter home to parents, but it might have been beneficial. Is this something parents can get involved with and help with? Wouldn't it be nice for them to see what their kids are interested in and passionate about?)

Steps to Success

1. Prepare yourself as a facilitator. (See what others have done and connect if you can. Be a model for your students and get started with your own 20% Time.)
2. Preparing the class. (Have your ducks all in a row before starting. There should be a way for them to share and collaborate if need be, and a way for them to understand all the reasons you have for them to do this project.)
3. A plan. (When and how often will they have 20% Time?)
4. Conferences. (Plan to meet with all of your students one-on-one about their learning.)
5. Sharing. (Build in time for students to share with each other regularly.)
6. Reflections. (The meta-cognitive piece is so important! Students should recognize what they have been learning.)
7. Facilitating success and failure. (Many students will "fail" to reach lofty goals they set for themselves. But this is not a failure; it is the best learning experience to have. Make sure you share great stories about success and failure while following your passions.)
8. Presentations and feedback. (As students present to the class they should hear feedback from peers and you. Don't let the learning stop with the presentation.)

The "This Sounds Great, But . . ." Group

I know, I know: 20% Time can seem like just another fad in education. There are plenty of excuses and reasons to NOT do it in your class/school. I want to take the time to dispel a few of the MYTHS that may arise about 20% Time. If you still have questions about running this type of project at your school, please feel free to send me an email to discuss in more detail.[2]

Debunking the Myths

Myth #1: 20% Time Isn't Supporting My Curriculum

Chances are you don't have the same curriculum I did, but most of us have similar types of curriculum. For instance, most Language Arts classes read a mixture of fiction and non-fiction texts. Many times teachers are pressed to find non-fiction pieces to support their class. Why find one non-fiction article for the entire class to read when your students can find many articles that they would actually want to read!? You can cover the same reading, writing, speaking, and listening skills during 20% Time that you cover during your normal curriculum. In fact, this can even enrich some of those learning experiences.

Maybe you are an elementary teacher, or middle school teacher who covers a wide range of subjects. Have you ever heard of an "I-Search" paper? Do your students write research papers in your Science, Math, or Social Studies classes? Do you teach health and cover a wide range of topics? Let 20% Time make learning be a personal experience for these students, and one that they'll want to share with you, their classmates, and their family.

Too often we cover a wide "breadth" of topics in one subject area, but fail to get into a depth of knowledge (check out Webb's Depth of Knowledge). 20% Time allows students to go into depth on a topic that they are already interested in, so they are intrinsically motivated to learn.

Myth #2: 20% Time Is Just for Enrichment Students

Yes, this could be a great way to motivate enrichment students, and something to add to an enrichment curriculum, but it should not be limited to those students.

Instead, 20% Time is actually beneficial to students with an IEP because the pace and level of the subject material can be tailored to their specific modifications. This is a valuable learning experience for every student.

Myth #3: The Common Core Anchors and Standards

Take a look at the Math CC Standards and the ELA CC Standards. Let me know what you think. But here are some of my personal favorites.

Common Core–20% Time Connections

Integration of Knowledge and Ideas

- CCSS.ELA-Literacy.CCRA.R.7 Integrate and evaluate content presented in diverse media and formats, including visually and quantitatively, as well as in words.

- CCSS.ELA-Literacy.CCRA.R.10 Read and comprehend complex literary and informational texts independently and proficiently. "Students also acquire the habits of reading independently and closely, which are essential to their future success."
- CCSS.ELA-Literacy.RST.6-8.3 Follow precisely a multistep procedure when carrying out experiments, taking measurements, or performing technical tasks.

Research to Build and Present Knowledge

- CCSS.ELA-Literacy.WHST.6-8.7 Conduct short research projects to answer a question (including a self-generated question), drawing on several sources and generating additional related, focused questions that allow for multiple avenues of exploration.
- CCSS.ELA-Literacy.WHST.6-8.8 Gather relevant information from multiple print and digital sources, using search terms effectively; assess the credibility and accuracy of each source; and quote or paraphrase the data and conclusions of others while avoiding plagiarism and following a standard format for citation.
- CCSS.ELA-Literacy.WHST.6-8.9 Draw evidence from informational texts to support analysis reflection, and research.

Range of Writing

- CCSS.ELA-Literacy.WHST.6-8.10 Write routinely over extended time frames (time for reflection and revision) and shorter time frames (a single sitting or a day or two) for a range of discipline-specific tasks, purposes, and audiences.

Standards for Mathematical Practice

- CCSS.Math.Practice.MP3 Construct viable arguments and critique the reasoning of others. Mathematically proficient students understand and use stated assumptions, definitions, and previously established results in constructing arguments. They make conjectures and build a logical progression of statements to explore the truth of their conjectures. They are able to analyze situations by breaking them into cases, and can recognize and use counterexamples. They justify their conclusions, communicate them to others, and respond to the arguments of others. They reason inductively about data, making plausible arguments that take into account the context from which the data arose. Mathematically proficient students are also able to compare the effectiveness of two plausible arguments, distinguish correct logic or reasoning from that which is flawed, and—if there is a flaw in an argument—explain what it is. Elementary students can construct arguments using concrete referents such as objects, drawings, diagrams, and actions. Such arguments can make sense and be correct, even though they are not generalized or made formal until later grades. Later, students learn to determine domains to which an argument applies. Students at all grades can listen or read the arguments of others, decide whether they make sense, and ask useful questions to clarify or improve the arguments.[3]

- CCSS.Math.Practice.MP4 Model with mathematics. Mathematically proficient students can apply the mathematics they know to solve problems arising in everyday life, society, and the workplace. In early grades, this might be as simple as writing an addition equation to describe a situation. In middle grades, a student might apply proportional reasoning in order to plan a school event or analyze a problem in the community. By high school, a student might use geometry to solve a design problem or use a function to describe how one quantity of interest depends on another. Mathematically proficient students who can apply what they know are comfortable making assumptions and approximations to simplify a complicated situation, realizing that these may need revision later. They are able to identify important quantities in a practical situation and map their relationships using such tools as diagrams, two-way tables, graphs, flowcharts, and formulas. They can analyze those relationships mathematically to draw conclusions. They routinely interpret their mathematical results in the context of the situation and reflect on whether the results make sense, possibly improving the model if it has not served its purpose.[4]

In any case, you can NOT use the Common Core standards (or any set of learning standards) as an excuse to dismiss 20% Time in your class/school. If anything, it ties in perfectly to many of these new standards.

Myth #4: Parents Won't Get Behind It

This myth can be true at the beginning of the project. Parents may be wary that this isn't good use of instructional time. Some parents might even think you aren't doing your job. That is, until your students prove them and everyone else wrong. If you truly believe in inquiry-driven learning this can be one of the biggest obstacles to overcome in some school settings. In order to combat it, make sure you are open and up front with parents. Share examples of what students in other places have done, and make sure you let them know how you are supporting, teaching, and facilitating their students throughout the process.

Myth #5: Administration Won't Let It Happen

Similar to parents, this can be a major obstacle in the beginning. Again, make sure you show your administrators the research behind inquiry-driven learning. You can recommend books and articles on user-generated learning. Show them examples of past 20% and Genius Hour projects. Heck, buy them a copy of *Drive* by Daniel Pink . . . it'll be worth the $14.99.

Show how this type of innovation in learning can lead students down the path of achievement. Be honest about your purpose for the project in your class, and maybe connect them to other administrators who have supervised over projects like this in their own school.

If you are still feeling a bit uneasy about starting this project, get connected on Twitter during #GeniusHour chats. Or join a 20% Time in Education community on Google+ to talk with other educators. Whatever you do, make sure that these myths don't stop you from starting.

The "That's Crazy!" Group

If you read the first and second parts of this chapter then what is probably stopping you is attitude. There are three problems I see that are all interconnected and they start with how we learn in school.

> Problem #1: Students don't get to choose their learning experiences in school.
>
> Problem #2: Many students leave school (graduate or drop out) without a true passion for something in life.
>
> Problem #3: Many adults work at jobs they don't like, in fields they are not passionate about, just to get by.

Can you see the direct correlation between each problem? Too often the system of schooling sends students down a path to follow direction and be rewarded. Do we teach our best students to just play the "game" of school? Using 20% Time combats this issue by still providing rigor in school, but with chosen content. When facilitated correctly, it allows students to first find, and then develop, their passions.

Companies like 3M, Google, Hewlett-Packard, and Yahoo! have used some form of 20% Time to spur innovation. And guess what . . . it worked! According to Marissa Meyer, almost HALF of Google's products originated from 20% Time, including the widely popular Gmail.

But, don't just listen to me. Read the next few chapters and see how inquiry-driven learning and 20% Time is working in schools today. Read about how a tenth grade student cloned a carnivorous plant during his 20% Time. Listen to a seventh grader talk about equal rights in his school. Watch how a Facebook page created to take compliments for students around the school turned into a movement.

These stories are real and the learning is powerful. Our students don't need to wait till they leave school to make an impact on the world around them.

Notes

1 *Wall Street Journal* 2010.
2 I'd love to connect! Email me at ajjuliani@gmail.com.
3 www.corestandards.org/Math/Practice.
4 www.corestandards.org/Math/Practice.

20% Time and Genius Hour Project Handout

THE GENIUS PROJECT: AUTONOMY, MASTERY, AND PURPOSE

DOCUMENTING THE PROCESS

PROJECT PITCH (10%): PRESENTED 2/20

- Three-Slide PowerPoint
    - Motivation
    - Timeline and resources
    - Goal
- Three minutes. Be prepared with an effective/refined script and delivery.
- A three to five sentence typed explanation
- Q & A

BLOG (MINIMALLY SIX ENTRIES): DUE DAY SIX OF CYCLE (50%)

- Blogger.com (post your blog address to the appropriate Moodle forum)
- Do not include last names in the blog
- *Measurable Goals:* Must be part of your first blog
    - What are your goals?
    - How will you measure your progress/achievement?
- Document your time and your *readings*, which should encompass at least twenty-five percent of your time
    - Include citations from specific sources
    - Provide an explanation of how these have informed your project
- Discuss your *discoveries and setbacks.*
    - What have you learned about your project?
    - What have you learned about yourself?
    - Where do you go from here?
- *Other:* pictures/graphs/charts, videos, links, etc.
- Establish your voice . . .
- Comment on three other people's blogs. Be sure to indicate on your own blog where you left comments.

VIDEO BLOG (10%): DUE BY 3/19

- An additional entry . . .
- Use Vimeo. Embed in Blogger.
- Two minutes
- What/who has inspired you?
- How have your readings/resources informed your approach?
- Anything else?

TED TALK (30%): WEEK OF APRIL 1ST

- Four to five minutes
- *Visual component*
    - o PPT, Prezi, other?
    - o Creative and supplemental. *You* drive the presentation, not the visual.
- *Content*:
    - o Inspire through your passion
    - o Show your **product**
    - o Explain your process
    - o What is your purpose? What should your audience take away from your project?
- *Organization*: hook, transitions, logical order, effective conclusion
- *Delivery*: refined, poised, and enthusiastic

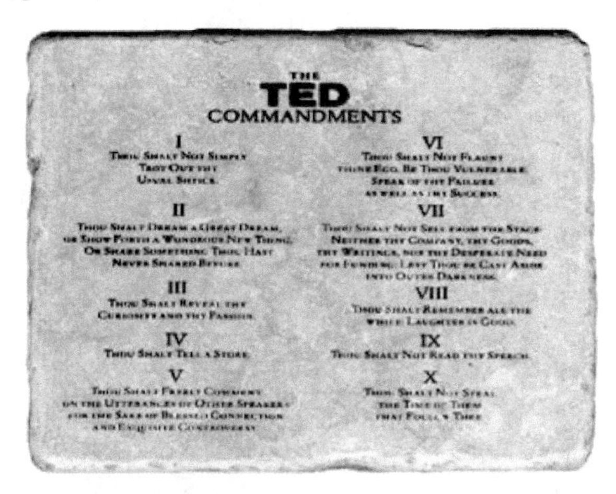

- **Dream big.** Strive to create the best talk you have ever given. Reveal something never seen before. Do something the audience will remember forever. Share an idea that could change the world.
- **Show us the real you.** Share your passions, your dreams . . . and also your fears. Be vulnerable. Speak of failure as well as success.
- **Make the complex plain.** Don't try to dazzle intellectually. Don't speak in abstractions. Explain! Give examples. Tell stories. Be specific.
- **Connect with people's emotions.** Make us laugh! Make us cry!
- **Don't flaunt your ego.** Don't boast. It's the surest way to switch everyone off.
- **No selling from the stage!** Unless we have specifically asked you to, do not talk about your company or organization. And don't even think about pitching your products or services or asking for funding from the stage.
- **Feel free to comment on other speakers' talks**, to praise or to criticize. Controversy energizes! Enthusiastic endorsement is powerful!
- **Don't read your talk.** Notes are fine. But if the choice is between reading or rambling, then read!
- **End your talk on time.** Doing otherwise is to steal time from the people that followyou. We won't allow it.
- **Rehearse your talk** in front of a trusted friend . . . for timing, for clarity, for impact.

Courtesy of Ryan Perlman and Chris McDaniels

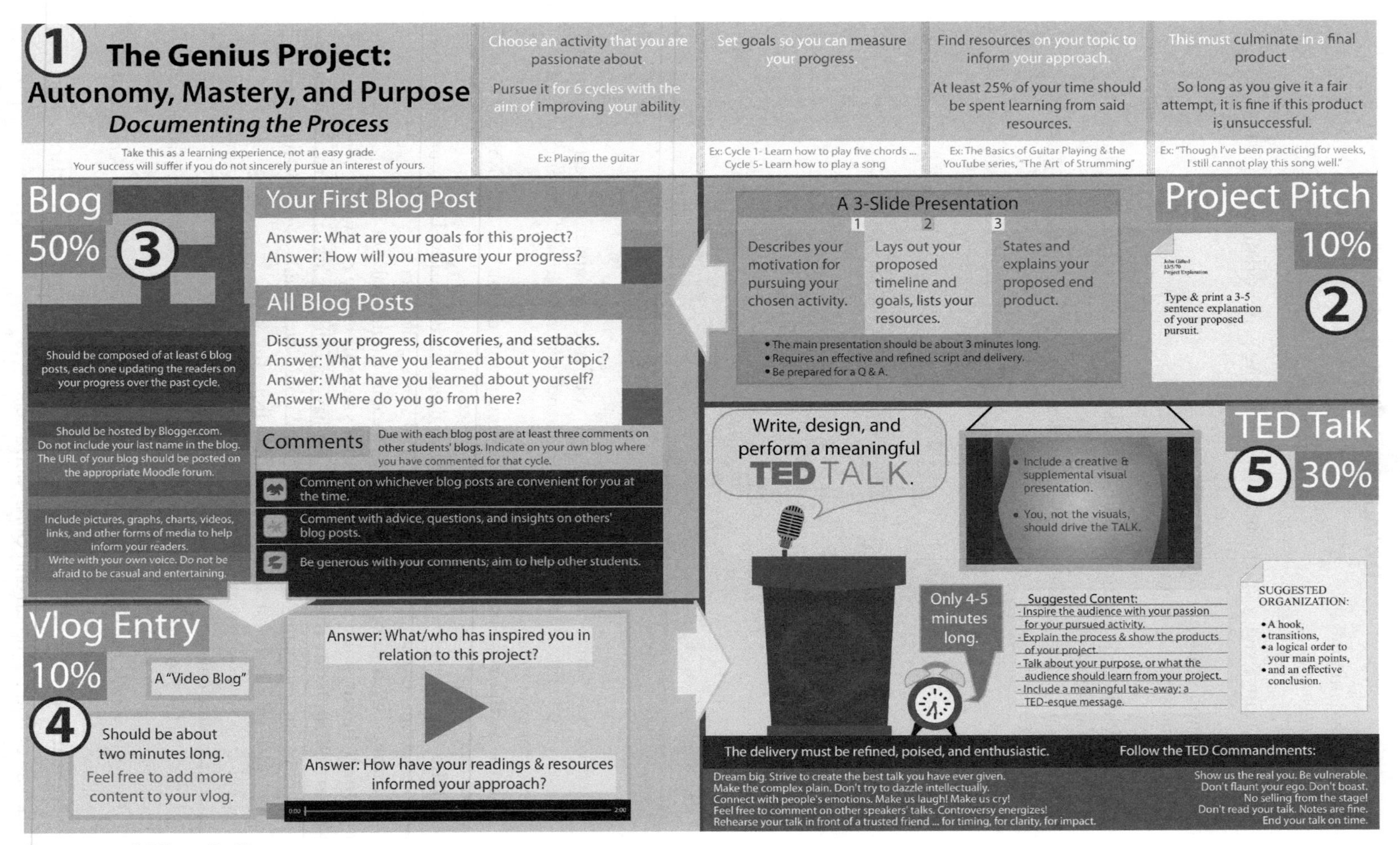

Courtesy of Ethan Reilly

CHAPTER

5

Genius Hour for Elementary Students

This chapter covers the work of Denise Krebs, Gallit Zvi, Joy Kirr, and Hugh McDonald as they bring Genius Hour into the elementary classroom. Inspired by Daniel Pink and Angela Maiers, these teachers give young students the opportunity to find their passions and explore their true interests. Their stories are inspiring, and the step-by-step guide on how to run 20% Time at an elementary level is easy to follow and implement.

A Moment of Genius

Denise Krebs had been teaching since 1986. In that time, she witnessed a variety of educational change, both in policy and practice in her middle school. Although Denise was constantly striving to be an innovative teacher with "out-of-the-box" thinking, it wasn't until she saw a tweet from Angela Maiers in late 2011 that real genius struck.

After seeing that tweet, Denise did a Google search for Genius Hour and Dan Pink's blog post, "The Genius Hour: How 60 minutes a week can electrify your job," came up. That's all she needed. It was the kind of learning experience she had always wanted to provide for her students. They've been doing it ever since.

Genius Hour is student-driven, passion-based learning. Very simply, it is a time when learners are asked what they want to learn, and the teacher gets out of their way. Denise's students do Genius Hour each week—students choose what they want to learn and then produce something to show their learning. Students are given time to learn what they want about the large unit at hand or how they will show understanding of one of the content area standards (in social studies or science in my classes). They practice researching techniques, close reading, and presenting, which are all standards we need to teach. However, the content is chosen based on their own interests.

Genius Hour in the classroom could have stopped right there. It could have been bottled up inside Denise's classroom, but the idea started to spread like wildfire. Gallit Zvi and Hugh McDonald were both connected educators who worked right down the hall from each other in the Surrey School District. Hugh

mrsdkrebs Denise Krebs
I want to hear more! RT @AngelaMaiers: LOVE This! We need to have a "**genius hour**" in school- for teachers and students! #authorspeak11
22 hours ago

AngelaMaiers Angela Maiers
LOVE This! We need to have a "**genius hour**" in school- for teachers and students! #authorspeak11
23 hours ago

Figure 5.1

and Gallit saw Denise's tweet and immediately jumped in. Following Denise's lead on connecting the idea to the classroom, Hugh and Gallit got started with their students in late 2011. The movement was spreading, and the students were once again enthralled with learning.

During the spring of 2012 the "Genius Hour" Wikispace was created, and the #geniushour Twitter chat started. The Wikispace served as a place for educators to share the motivation for Genius Hour, how they were running it in their classroom, and provided great resources for making it a success with students. The chat allowed educators to talk and connect with each other at any time online. Soon teachers like Joy Kirr got involved. Joy was looking for an overhaul of the way her ELA department tackled independent reading. As she says,

> I was so tired of doing more work than the students, with quarterly book projects being due the week of grades, and knowing many students didn't actually read any of the book. So . . . researching anything of their choice? Sounds like independent reading to me! I was hooked on the idea that students could pursue their own learning.[1]

Hugh McDonald echoed Joy's feelings in the "Genius Hour Manifesto":

> The joy in my students' eyes and the eyes of the teachers in my school when they saw my students at work on their initial Genius Hour projects was priceless. Genius Hour as an idea gives autonomous personalized learning time out of every week to students to question, think, learn, and explore the things they loved and were curious about. This was something special that engaged learners like nothing I had seen before. The learning atmosphere felt amazing. I could walk down the hall and ask Gallit a question and return to see them all still on task, questioning, driving their own learning, and having fun being curious. It was an amazing feeling as a teacher to see your students excited about learning. By modeling what

a learner thinks about when they are learning I was seeing individualized, personal, and passionate learning taking place before my eyes by a classroom full of 12 and 13 year-olds.[2]

In this chapter, you'll see how to prepare your class (and yourself) for Genius Hour, what teachable moments can happen during the project, how to assess student learning, and ways to connect with other elementary and middle school teachers running Genius Hour in their classrooms. It is truly personalized learning and so vital because as one of Gallit's students, Morgan, pointed out, "you don't want to learn your teacher's passion, you want to learn your own passion."

Preparing Your Class

Introducing the project to your students is one of the most exciting, and important, moments for Genius Hour. Most of your students may be confused about inquiry-based learning. For the majority of their schooling lives, they've been told:

1. What to do (write a paper on Volcanic eruptions).
2. How to do it (it should be five paragraphs long with an intro, three body paragraphs, and conclusion).
3. Why they should do it (you'll be receiving a grade on how well you complete the task).

You'll be telling students:

1. They can learn what they want
2. In a variety of ways
3. Because they are interested and passionate about the material.

Many Genius Hour teachers start with the why. This can be done through showing inspirational videos and presentations, or by showing what other students have done in Genius Hour. Similarly, teachers in my school loved talking about the research behind Malcolm Gladwell's "10,000" hours. It states that to become a true expert you need to spend around 10,000 hours practicing or learning. My favorite way to introduce Genius Hour is for students to write a list of what they'd rather be doing right now than being in school. Usually you'll get lots of answers involving sports, television, games, hanging out, eating, or sleeping. Then I ask them to write a list of what they are interested about in this world. I give them some examples I have, such as, "Why are yawns contagious?" and "Is it possible for a 5'7 man to dunk a basketball?" The final question is for them to look at what they like doing (the first list) and mash it up with something they are interested about (the second list). This is a potential topic for Genius Hour.

Denise has students who are having difficulty coming up with a topic to make lists of ten. Ten things they are good at, ten things they love to learn, ten things they love to do, ten things they wonder. She said:

> It's hard for some learners to make those lists. If most of what they have are consumer actions like playing video games, watching YouTube videos, etc., then I remind them that the historical etymology of the word *genius* is creative and productive, and that's what they are to be. I then help them develop a topic based on their lists. Perhaps, if they are all about video games, I might encourage them to download Scratch and make their own video game. Or, if they love to watch YouTube videos, then they can create their own film on something they care passionately about.[3]

More than anything, kids need to see why YOU are passionate about this project. They'll want to know what YOU would do with your hour of learning time. I highly recommend partaking in the project yourself and learning something new that you've always been interested in. This simple act will motivate your students to learn, and it will help you understand their point-of-view during the process.

Parents and Administration

Introducing the project to administration and parents is very different to the act of bringing it to your students. Depending on the type of school and community you work in, the reaction could be very different. However, remember two things when introducing to both of these groups: Be completely honest with your reasons and share results from others around the world.

Administrators may worry that this "free time" is really "wasted time." They are going to want to see what type of action you are doing during Genius Hour. Are you planning on sitting at your desk with your feet up, or are you going to be working with students one-on-one and in small groups? Are you going to be modeling what the learning should look like, or let them do whatever they want until it is time to present? Be careful that you are structuring this unstructured time. Each class should have a purpose, and be connected to a learning goal.

Teachers like Kevin Brookhouser created a letter to send home to parents explaining his reasons for running a 20% project in his class. At my school we invited parents and administrators to come and see the final presentations. Involve them in the process and they'll better understand what you are trying to accomplish.

During the Project

Create a list of quick ways to assess throughout the project. We spent a lot of time coming up with different benchmarks and checkpoints for the students. This is even more important with younger students as they need as much feedback as possible. Each checkpoint provides an opportunity for peer interaction and feedback.

Denise chooses to give students two periods a week, about 85 minutes, to work on their Genius Hour projects. Each Wednesday, students know that they can work on their project of choice. Oftentimes, these projects are long-term, going for four to six weeks. Other times, students choose a new project each week. For the most part, students bring their own supplies from home.

Denise makes it clear that,

> experience and reflection are key reasons to have genius hour. The experiential learning is engaging and gives students great joy. However, I also believe, as many have said, that experience without reflection does not produce real learning. Therefore, as part of Genius Hour, we do three things. We keep in mind the essential questions that we are trying to answer, we create products of our learning, and we make our learning visible by reflecting in a blog post about what we have learned at least each month.[4]

Gallit and Hugh have students work on their Genius Hour projects every Friday afternoon, and they present when they are ready. For some students that will be after one session and for some it will be after six. It really depends on what they are learning about and how they plan to present. Genius Hour is personalized learning and so they believe that presentations should take place when students feel ready, not because it is the "fourth" session. They check in with our students regularly and they will each blog about their progress as well.

I suggest thinking about a framework for your students to reach multiple checkpoints throughout the process:

1. First they must "pitch" their idea to the class. This allows them to take ownership of what they are working on, and explain why they chose this topic, what they are going to do, and how they will measure their success.
2. The next few checkpoints can be a series of blog posts. Students can share what they are learning (and creating) through written, audio, or video formats. Other students in their class can comment on their project as well.
3. During the project you should also make time for one-on-one conferences with the teacher or small group conferences. The teacher needs to be a guide on the side as much as possible.

4. Finally you'll want some sort of presentation. It can be formal or informal. But it must talk about the learning goals. Often students will feel like they failed . . . but failing in Genius Hour provides more learning than failing a test! Talk about the process and what you learned.

Allow students to share whenever they feel inspired, but the checkpoint makes it a priority to share their work even if they are a bit timid. Remember that not everything needs to be a fresh idea. Students can build upon previous ideas, and use examples from the lists of genius projects online. The goal is for our students to work on something that interests them; who cares if it isn't a new idea or topic?

Gathering Data

During Genius Hour you should spend time collecting data on your students' progress. How many words are they reading during research? How many words are they writing through journaling? What's the level of student engagement (focused and on-task) during a typical Genius Hour session? One of the best ways to exposing colleagues to this type of inquiry-based learning experience is to have them help out!

Have one of your colleagues, or administrators, come in and gather data. As a teacher this will help you understand how the time is being used, which students may need some redirecting, and how to tweak the experience so it is better down the road.

The Final Product

Each teacher who runs Genius Hour may have a different view on the "final product." The product can consist of three types: a tangible creation, a presentation, or a written piece. What kind of presentation you require from your students depends on the end goal. Did you focus Genius Hour on the "learning" or the "doing"? I always want to think of students as creators and makers. Even if they produce a set of poems, I want it to be packaged in a finished product (a book or eBook format). By focusing on the final creation or product, it allows the students to talk about the process—which is the most important aspect of Genius Hour.

Students will fail during Genius Hour. This is a good thing. Attacking the fundamental belief that "failure is bad" will be essential early on. Show your students how all of the great minds have spent time learning from failure. Great examples can be taken from Einstein, Franklin, Gates, Jobs, and even Michael Jordan. We need to fail, in order to become great. Have your students celebrate their failures, and share how they overcame each obstacle.

The real end-goal is hard to define. It's not about mastery, and it's not about a product. It's about growth. What do you understand now that you didn't before?

What are you able to do now that you could not four weeks ago? What do you know about the world that was a previous mystery? Inquiry allows our students to get excited about learning, and in the process they do amazing work, sometimes even innovative work. Remember to celebrate whatever they accomplish, even if it is the smallest amount of growth.

Classroom Application: Inspiration for Other Teachers Beginning Genius Hour

Gallit Zvi: I feel passionately about the need for education to become more individualized. I have spent the last two years researching motivation and personalized learning and there is much to be said for the connection between the two. I know that my students love when they are given choice in an assignment or project. They don't all learn the same and they don't all have the same interests. That is why Genius Hour is so key; it gives the students the freedom to choose not only the subject matter, but also the method their inquiry project is to use.

Hugh McDonald: I feel the importance of personalizing learning for students should be at the forefront of any discussion relating to education, and Genius Hour does that. We want to find ways to engage students as learners and creators of inquiry-driven content. The number one reason the students give for why they drop out was being bored with school! Yikes!! Inquiry-driven models like Genius Hour put the focus on how to question, persevere, and recognize the joy of learning more about their passions.

Joy Kirr: Get over it. It's not about YOU. It's about the kids. Maybe it's because I'm over 40 now that I want to say that?? But the politically correct way of saying it is: You don't know everything . . . What you know is not the end-all, be-all. You have a room full of curious, imaginative minds that you need to start utilizing to their fullest potential. If we want them to actually think . . . to make good choices in life, we have to start letting them make choices, fail, adapt, and make more choices. You need to be there for them when they do—as a guide, asking more questions, and getting them to think MORE. If you don't give them answers, you can bet that YOU will keep learning along with your students.

Connecting with Other Genius Hour Teachers and Students

Connecting online is the easiest way to find other teachers using Genius Hour in their classrooms. As mentioned above, you can check out the #geniushour hashtag and chat on Twitter, browse and contribute to the

Genius Hour Wikispace (http://geniushour.wikispaces.com/), or read the various blogs from Genius Hour teachers (most are listed on Joy Kirr's LiveBinder).

Another great way to connect is through Robyn Thiessen's "Global Genius Hour Project" Wiki, where teachers from around the world post what their students have been making and creating during Genius Hour. It's a great place for your students to share, and also to be inspired by what others students are doing with their "free" time during Genius Hour.

Education conferences everywhere have inquiry-based sessions, sometimes solely focused on Genius Hour or 20% Time. Edcamp and other "unconferences" are a perfect setting for teachers to share their experiences and spread the word.

Denise puts it perfectly.

> Genius hour is not a program. I believe it comes from a student-centered educational philosophy. When I became a connected educator, lifelong learner, and one who makes my own learning visible, that's when I wanted the same for my students. That's when I began actively teaching creativity and the skill of learning. That's when I started giving them time for genius hour.[5]

Notes

1 http://educationismylife.com/genius-hour-manifesto/.
2 Ibid.
3 Ibid.
4 Ibid.
5 Email correspondence.

Sample Parent Letter

Dear Parent/Guardian,

This year we are going to do something a bit different in our class. Each week we will be implementing a Genius Hour activity for our students. During Genius Hour students will be able to explore their interests and passions, and actually make something tangible to present to the class. This is not a new concept (although it may be for our school) and students from around the world are participating in Genius Hour and sharing their work with each other.

As a teacher, part of my job is to help your child develop academically and improve their critical thinking/higher-level thinking skills. Genius Hour gives our students that time: to create, to evaluate, to research, to synthesize, and to analyze. Because the topic is based on their interests, it comes from their own intrinsic motivations.

If you'd like to see what other teachers and students are doing around the world with Genius Hour please check out the following sites:

1. Genius Hour Main Wikispace: http://geniushour.wikispaces.com/
2. Global Genius Hour: http://theglobalgeniushourproject.wikispaces.com/
3. Choose2Matter: http://choose2matter.org/

We invite you to be a part of Genius Hour in our class. Please come in for a session and we will let you know when our students will be presenting what they have researched and created!

Thanks for your support!

CHAPTER

20% Time for Secondary Students

This chapter looks at the inquiry learning experience for high school and older students. Many of these students are beginning to think about their future and life after school. Often they struggle finding a passion and true purpose for their work. Experiences of 20% Time provide a avenue for students to explore their passions. This chapter provides a before, during, and after plan for teachers to use during 20% Time.

I was in a band for six years without ever being a musician: We were called the "25th Hour." I was a sixth grader when my best friend Jim started playing guitar. I bought one as well, and although I gave it a shot . . . my guitar ended up the same way as my clarinet, saxophone, and trumpet . . . dusty.

In seventh grade two of my friends were good enough to start thinking "band." I've been a bit outspoken my entire life and fit in nicely as a lead singer. We actually auditioned (in seventh grade) two drummers, with a girl winning out and joining the 25th Hour. Our fifth person played bass, and all of a sudden we had an actual band.

Now if you've ever been in a garage band before you'll realize that for us, it was a total experiment. Each practice, rehearsal, gig (yes, we played in some gigs), and recording session (two LPs) was a bizarre mix of fun, trial and error, and chaos. As we grew older, our expectations of ourselves rose, and our abilities also grew. It was still a ton of fun when we were in 11th and 12th grade, but a divide had been created.

The Passion Divide

You see, I wasn't as "passionate" about making music like three of my band mates were. I loved writing lyrics to new songs, enjoyed performing in front of people, and thought it was a ton of fun hanging out and practicing. I even spent a lot of time learning the technology behind the recording process . . . but this was not something I would continue after high school. It had a feeling of "being over" to me by the time I was a senior.

For three of my band mates, they had a real purpose for our band. They wanted to work in music and with music, while in college and preferably for the rest of their lives. They spent our practices and rehearsals playing with purpose, while I spent it having a good time. As a result they continued to improve as musicians and learn more about the process and industry. Two of them currently work in the music industry. Our drummer recently graduated from Harvard's Business School, and me . . . I went on to teach reading and writing to high school students with a new job now focused on technology.

The Difference Between Purpose and Passion

That's the difference between purpose and passion to me. Passion may get you going. It may have you fired up about a new project or opportunity. It may lead you to shout it from the mountain tops. But purpose is a different animal. It keeps you going when others fade away. It drives your everyday actions because there is a reason behind everything you do.

I've written and talked a lot about students finding their passions. About people finding their passions. And I do think that passion is a place to start, because it does lead to purpose. But, there is a reason Rick Warren's *The Purpose Driven Life* is the best-selling non-fiction hardback in history. We, as people, are looking for purpose in our lives. We are looking for self-actualization (as Abraham Maslow called it).

Passion may lead us to new experiences, but ultimately it should point us to purpose. For my band mates, the 25th Hour was the start of their journey in music. For me, it was the start of my journey with writing (although I didn't know it at the time). Interestingly, none of our "journeys" started in school. We used our free time to really find what we were passionate about, and to build a purpose into our learning and activities. This chapter is about giving students the opportunity to find passionate and purposeful learning experiences in school. After all, students spend about 1300 hours a year in the classroom—shouldn't we be using that time purposefully?

The Stages of Inquiry and Purpose

Professors at the Australian Catholic University have come up with an easy to use chart detailing the inquiry process. This chart has four stages. First, students and teachers must pose "Real Questions," that is the types of questions that lead to more questions and deeper understanding. After starting the process with a validated question, the second step is to "Find Resources." Students must identify which resources will be helpful and where they can find them. They must also validate the research and information. The third step is "Interpreting the Information," and students must connect the research and resources to their initial question. This leads to new understandings and several answers. The fourth and final step is to "Report Findings" to a specific audience. (See Figure 6.1.)[1]

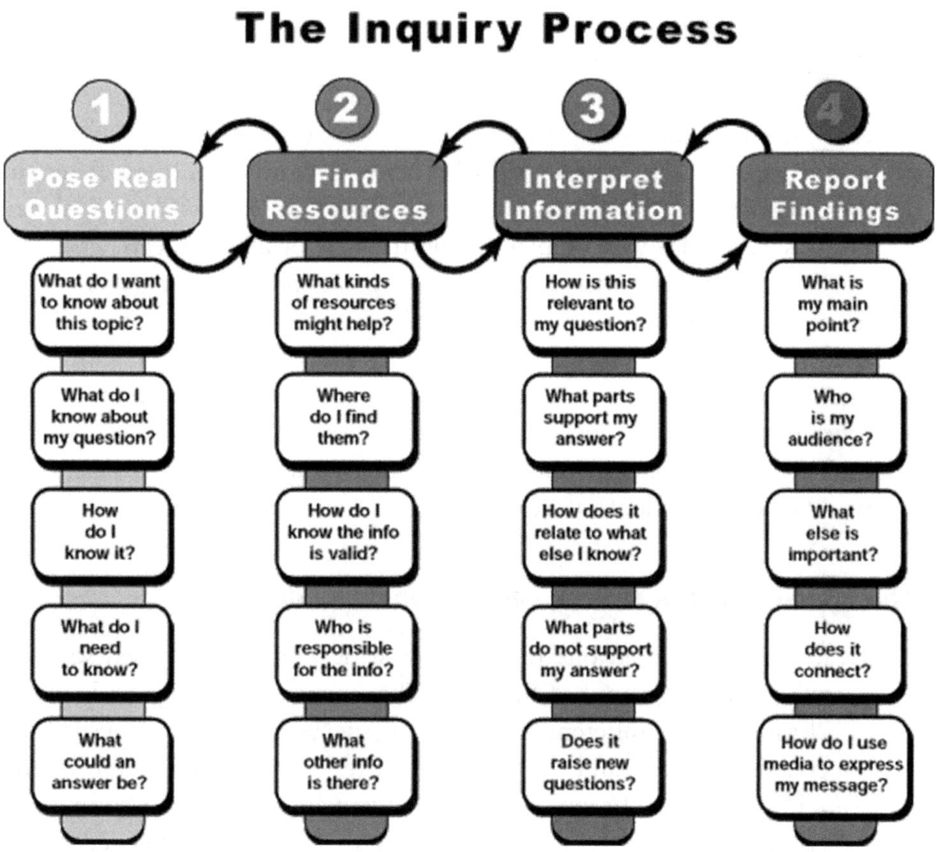

The Inquiry Process

1 Pose Real Questions	2 Find Resources	3 Interpret Information	4 Report Findings
What do I want to know about this topic?	What kinds of resources might help?	How is this relevant to my question?	What is my main point?
What do I know about my question?	Where do I find them?	What parts support my answer?	Who is my audience?
How do I know it?	How do I know the info is valid?	How does it relate to what else I know?	What else is important?
What do I need to know?	Who is responsible for the info?	What parts do not support my answer?	How does it connect?
What could an answer be?	What other info is there?	Does it raise new questions?	How do I use media to express my message?

Figure 6.1

Courtesy of YouthLearn Initiative at EDC, youthlearn.org

Our inquiry-based learning and 20% projects have a fifth step that is essential for student purpose. This step is "creation." When students ask the first question, they pose it with an understanding that it will lead to some type of finished product.

There was a ninth grade girl at my high school who knew what she wanted to do for her 20% project. She asked the question, "How can I learn sign-language?" This student was extremely busy in and out of school with challenging courses, extra-curricular activities, and responsibilities at home. She said in her final presentation that it was amazing to have this time to learn sign-language. However, she did not come and present to her classmates what she learned . . . she presented a final product: a song in sign-language.

As she told the story of why she wanted to learn sign-language, we learned that her young cousin was deaf. She had always wanted to learn sign-language, and this 20% project gave her the perfect opportunity. What she presented was a song in sign-language that she would also perform for her cousin. As she sang the song in sign, almost half the class was choked up with emotion. She had purpose in her learning, and it showed.

This story is one of many where students took an opportunity to learn what they wanted, and turned it into a successful product. However, this does not always happen. There are many students who have trouble finding their interests. They have difficulty separating their interests from their passions. And ultimately they struggle to create a final product with much purpose. After running these inquiry-based projects in my own classroom, and working with teachers in my school who were implementing the idea of 20% projects, I began to see trends in successful projects. Similarly, the great community of teachers running inquiry and passion projects has shared what has worked in their classrooms. Below you'll find a framework for inquiry-based learning that allows for (and often requires) failure. This, above all else, is the key factor in inquiry leading to innovation. Students must fail often, learn from those failures, and apply those lessons to their work. It's only when we focus our "assessment" on growth that we actually see students succeeding beyond their imaginations.

The Building Blocks of 20% Time in the Classroom

John Wooden created one of the most widely shared and used strategies for growth in his "Pyramid of Success." The winningest college basketball coach of all-time gave a different definition of success than what is usually shared: "Success is piece of mind which is a direct result in self-satisfaction in knowing you did your best to become the best that you are capable of becoming."

The Pyramid itself is a dynamic view of all the traits needed to succeed not only in sports, but also in life. The bottom level includes industriousness, friendship, loyalty, cooperation, and enthusiasm. The next level includes self-control, alertness, initiative, and intentness. The middle row contains conditioning, skill, and team spirit. The second highest level focuses on poise and confidence. Finally, the top of the pyramid is met with competitive greatness. It does not end with "winning" but instead with the act of competing to your highest possible level.

As a coach I've used Wooden's "Pyramid of Success" with many of my teams. My players can see how each building block in the pyramid leads to the next level of success. And each block has an important place in reaching greatness. The last time I gave this to a group of my players, my eyes were opened during a brief conversation.

Our team captain raised his hand during the meeting and asked me, "Coach, I know a lot of guys on the team are just starting to play lacrosse. There's no way we can all have the same skill. How can we ever get to that next level of confidence?"

I thought about his question for a second. It seemed appropriate and he was spot on with the analysis. Yet, my captain was missing the most crucial idea behind this pyramid.

Figure 6.2

Courtesy of Ralph Paglia from www.automotivedigitalmarketing.com/photo/john-woodens-pyramid-of

I said,

> You're right. Not everyone has the same skill, and we can't catch all the new players up this season. But as a team, our overall skill can continue improving if each player keeps getting better. You may be better than some of the players on our team, but guys in college are much better than you at lacrosse. What we are aiming to do, is continue growing in each of these areas. That way, our competitive greatness can lead to more and more success.

When teachers think about students doing a 20% Time project, or inquiry-based learning, we tend to think about what skills our students currently possess. We may expect more from a straight "A" student than we do from an average "C" student. Not only is this thinking completely backwards, it misses the point!

Inquiry-based learning (especially at the high school level) is about providing time for students to grow as learners, individuals, and creators. They may not be a straight "A" student, but their inquiry project will blow you away.

I've identified six building blocks that lead students down a path of growth in their 20% Time project. Teachers should focus on these six areas in the planning, preparation, and implementation parts of inquiry-based learning. These building blocks have been used by teachers for a long time, and the most successful teachers know to look for them on a daily basis.

The six building blocks for inquiry-based success are:

1. Passion
2. Purpose
3. Ownership (Autonomy)
4. Sharing
5. Creating and Making
6. Reflection

Passion

As I mentioned earlier, it all starts with a passion and true intrinsic motivation. As Oprah Winfrey has stated: "Passion is energy. Feel the power that comes from focusing on what excites you." Once students are able to identify a true passion, their academic energy will skyrocket. If you've never given choice in your classroom, you may have missed witnessing this type of effect take place. However, once a student is motivated by himself, he is driven to succeed on an entirely different level.

Purpose

Passion without purpose is like a car without a destination. Sure, it's fun to drive the first time you get into it, but after a while the act of driving becomes rather mundane. There is no reason to drive, and no end goal. Purpose gives your passion an outlet. Albert Einstein wrote a good bit about passion and purpose as an outlet: "We act as though comfort and luxury were the chief requirements of life, when all that we need to make us happy is something to be enthusiastic about." Purpose drives the beginning research and the final creation.

Ownership (Autonomy)

A popular word among inquiry-based teachers is "autonomy." The word is defined as "freedom from external control or influence; independence." Giving students a sense of autonomy is one of the first steps to a successful project. However, this type of freedom can also be misconstrued as a path to doing nothing. Instead, I'd much rather focus my students' attention on "owning" their project. It is their work, their time, their failures, their successes, and their growth. Similarly, ownership allows for partnerships. You can "co-own" a project, which many students choose to do, but autonomy is restricted to the individual.

Sharing

The second level of building blocks for inquiry-based projects starts with sharing. Some believe sharing is a one-way street, but you must make it apparent that in every sharing action there is a sharer, and a receiver. Students will first be receivers of information. Millions of people have "shared" their thoughts, research, and resources online. This research is what drives the next stage of creation. However, after researching students must also share their findings with classmates and hopefully the world. I highly recommend students blogging about their experience and findings. This takes "ownership" to the next level because it is sharing progress, failures, and successes with a larger community. In turn, the students will benefit the community through their sharing, much as they were benefited by people sharing before them.

Creating and Making

Creation is a funny word. We usually make it out to be something BIG. The creating piece of an inquiry project is where we see innovation come into the equation. Students understand their initial question. They have a fueling passion to do something, and their purpose should be a final product . . . or creation. That product can be a song (as I mentioned before) or a book, or a car motor, or a computer, or a computer game, and the list goes on. This is the building block that has the most frustration attached to it. Students often want to make a product that is beyond their current abilities. Let them try. They'll learn from failures and do amazing work when their back is against the wall. The final product is both a challenge of the mind and the innovative process. Remind them to have fun, and to keep bouncing back from missteps.

Reflection

Reflection, by definition, is a serious thought or consideration. Although true reflection comes by expressing this idea in more than a thought. In 20% Time projects you can have students reflect at various points: reflect on their question, reflect on their passions, reflect on their product, reflect on their research, and reflect on their experience. Students can reflect through their writing (I highly recommend student blogging throughout the process), podcasts, videos, and the final presentation. Reflection is where students can self-assess their own growth. It is also a time for them to assess learning.

Each of these building blocks for inquiry-based learning is essential to the process and success of every student. As you begin to plan and implement 20% Time take time to think about how each student can effectively find their passion, develop a learning purpose, take ownership of their project, share what they are learning, create something special, and reflect on the experience.

Before the Project

"Failing to prepare is preparing to fail."

John Wooden

Now that we've identified the six areas that drive student growth during an inquiry-based project, it's time to prepare our students, classroom, and learning community. Although I'm tempted to tell you to "just do it," it's wise to take a few specific measures in preparation.

Connect it to the Curriculum

Administration, parents, and your colleagues will all immediately ask the same question when hearing about a 20% project: How does it fit into the curriculum? You should have this answer ready. For my English class, we connected it to the curriculum through non-fiction texts. Students read a lot during 20% Time. They also spend a long amount of time researching through video and audio texts. The Common Core standards (see Chapter 9) are big on research and analysis. They also call for more non-fiction texts. Using 20% Time gave my students a way to read more non-fiction, but it was based on their interests. Be sure to make a connection to your curriculum in some meaningful manner.

Learn from the Community

Read as many 20% teacher blogs and inquiry-based teaching experiences as you can before embarking on your own project. Each teacher has their own unique twist on this type of inquiry-based project, from Kevin Brookhouser's "Bad Idea Factory" to Ryan Perlman's search for "10,000 hours." Take, use, and remix what others have done into your own project. Just be sure to make it fit with your class needs above all else.

Structure Your Time

You'll need to have a set schedule for 20% Time in your class. Students will be more productive when they can prepare ahead of time for this unstructured time. You'll also need to plan out the milestones of the project (see sample handout at the end of this chapter) to keep students working at a good pace.

Get Your Pitch Ready . . .

The best pitch you'll have to get ready is the one for your students. It is one of the best experiences to introduce this project. Revel in the moment. Take in the sideways glances, open stares, and confused faces. You should also have a pitch ready for colleagues, parents, and administration. They are going to ask questions, and you may want to present the project to these stakeholders before the students.

During the Project

> "It's the little details that are vital. Little things make big things happen."
>
> John Wooden

After you present the project to your class you'll inevitably have a handful (if not half) of the students who have no idea what they are passionate about. This can be disheartening, but it is also one of the reasons inquiry-based projects are needed in our schools. You see, I'm the type of person who is interested in a million different things (maybe not a million, but close!). However, although I'm interested in Icelandic elves, the different types of cheese steaks, hacking Kickstarter projects, and fantasy football . . . none of those interests are my passions. I spent time on all of those interests in some way recently. But I may not spend time on any of those this entire week. **This was a huge revelation to me: Just because I'm interested in something, doesn't make it a potential "passion" of mine.**

Some people know what their passion in life is intrinsically. Others, like myself, have hundreds of interests that may distract us from our real passions in life. In order for you to sift through the noise and interests in your life to find your ultimate passion, follow these strategies:

Take Notice of What You Do When No One Is "Telling You What to Do"

This is a big one. What types of activities do you do when you are not working, learning, or being told what to do? To dig even deeper, ask yourself these questions:

- What do I do on weekend mornings?
- What do I do after dinner during the weekday?
- What do I do when I have time off work/school?
- What do I do when I'm sick and at home?
- What do I do late at night/early in the morning?

Then you are going to have to analyze the results. Chances are, many of these activities will be **consumption** (watching TV, playing a video game, using an app, reading a book/magazine/blog) or they'll be **communication** (hang out with friends, talk with friends, chat online, etc.).

If there is anything you do during these times that is considered "creating" or "making" be sure to star that on your list. Maybe it is writing, or working on your car, or putting together a stereo system, or making a dance/song, or doing a craft (digital or not). We'll revisit these items later down the list.

Take Notice Of What You Do When You Are "Supposed to Be Doing Something Else"

If you are anything like me, then you get off-task all the time. In fact, I really should be revising a chapter of my book right now, but inspiration hit and I wanted to write this post. Just as we did above, take note of what types of activities you do when you are "supposed to be doing something else." This could be at work, at school, or at home.

We all have responsibilities and priorities in our life. We have things we "need to get done." However, when we put those responsibilities or priorities to the side to work on something else, that is a telling sign of our passions. Again, you should make a list and separate it between consumption activities, communication activities, and creating/making activities.

What Types of Information Do You Read and Watch?

Maybe all you read is sports magazines, and all you watch is ESPN. Maybe all you read is fashion blogs, and all you watch is Project Runway re-runs. Or maybe (like me) you read and watch a variety of things. That's fine. Either way you should make a list.

We consume what we are interested in, but often it is a way to relax. Now think about what types of information that you consume get you pumped up and ready to go! Those need to be starred on your list.

Create Your Own "March Madness Interests" Bracket

It may sound silly, but I like it better than a Venn diagram (ugh). Print out a blank March Madness bracket like the one in Figure 6.3, and fill it with your interests that were compiled from our previous three strategies.

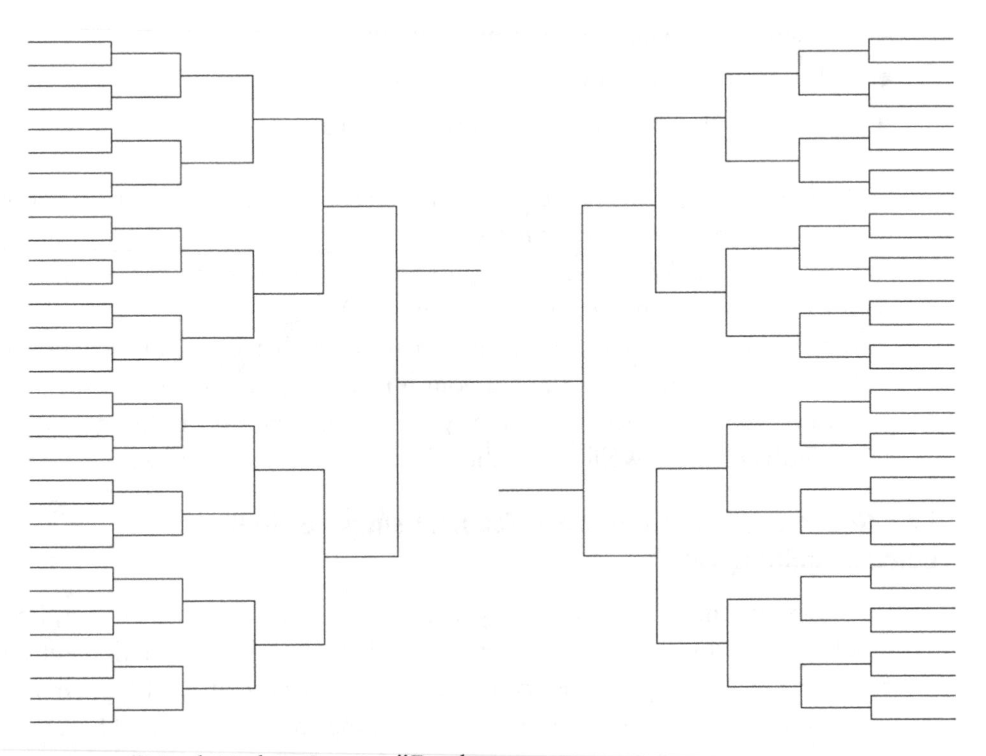

Figure 6.3 "March Madness Interests" Bracket

Now start to eliminate interests based on what you would like to spend time doing if you won the lottery and could do anything! This is a fun way to make yourself come up with answers to tough questions.

Give Yourself a Trial Period

You've narrowed down your interests into viable passions. However, it's still difficult to pin down which interests are actually your true passions. So give yourself a trial period. Take each of your "Final Four" interests/passions and spend as much time as you can working and creating with that passion that week.

During this trial period, note which of your passions put you into a state of "flow." In a state of "flow" you'll lose all sense of time, because you are so focused on the task at hand. This is my best recommendation for a deciding factor of which interest is actually a passion.

Get Started!

What do I mean by "get started"? This is where your passion begins to have purpose. Passion may get you going. It may have you fired up about a new project or opportunity. It may lead you to shout it from the mountain tops. But purpose is a different animal. It keeps you going when others fade away. It drives your everyday actions because there is a reason behind everything you do.

If you find that you are passionate about fashion and writing, then start a fashion blog where you are able to write about new trends. The blog will give your actions a purpose, and drive your creating. A student of mine wanted to learn sign-language, but her purpose was to perform a song in sign for her deaf cousin . . . that purpose drove her learning and made her successful.

It can be difficult finding a passion, but when you get started with an idea that has purpose, you'll always be moving in the right direction.

When your students come up with a passion they truly care about, it will be evident in their work and demeanor. They'll be excited to come into class. They'll want to talk and share about their research, project, and final product. If you have a student who is still having an apathetic view on inquiry-based learning, have them team up with another student. Passion is contagious. Let it fly around your classroom.

The Final Product and Presentation

> "It's what you learn after you know it all that counts."
>
> John Wooden

The journey may be more important than the final destination, but the final product and presentation can provide a unique learning experience for all of your students. I've had my students post their final project presentations online so all my classes could watch. I've also seen teachers in my school get the auditorium for a week and have students' present TED-style five to ten minute talks on their project. You need to find what type of medium and time will work in your school.

Keep in mind the final product should be:

- Based on their initial question: Each product doesn't have to be "unique" but it should be built out of their curiosity and passion.
- Tangible: It does not need to be a physical product. But there should be a tangible aspect where the audience can see what was made, created, or produced.
- Flawed: Set this as an expectation going in. We know every project won't be perfect. It does not need to be perfect. I had a student perform a song and really struggle to get through it on stage. Afterwards we saw how hard she had worked, and gave a long standing applause.

See what other Genius Hour and 20% Time teachers have done on the Genius Hour Resource page: http://geniushour.wikispaces.com/ or at Kate Petty's site http://20timeineducation.com/.

After the Project

Provide a number of opportunities for students to reflect after the project. Allow them to write about their experience (possibly a final blog post), post their work online in a public space to share (Choose2Matter.org), and share with parents and peers.

One of my students put it all in perspective during their reflection:

> I didn't know what to think when I started this project. In fact, I didn't really know how to think. I'm a great student, but sometimes I felt like I was never really learning anything. This project challenged me like nothing I've ever done before. I put a lot of stress on myself to do something great, but it was through failing (a number of times!) that I learned the Most.

Give students this opportunity and you'll learn a lot about them, they'll learn a lot about each other, and most importantly they'll learn a lot about themselves.

Note

1 From "Inquiry Learning" Blog http://s00077474.wordpress.com/the-inquiry-process-diagram/

GRIT Rubric

Grading these projects is always difficult. In fact, in my initial project I did not grade my students' presentations and final product. Instead, I focused on grading the process. A great way to grade students is to use the GRIT rubric developed by the College Track program in San Francisco. "College Track is an afterschool, college preparatory program that works to increase high school graduation, college eligibility and enrollment, and college graduation rates in under-resourced communities." The program is amazing, but what blew me away was the GRIT acronym and student rubric. College Track has broken the word "grit" down to four factors: Guts, Resilience, Integrity, and Tenacity. From their site:

> It takes a lot beyond academic readiness to succeed in college. Tackling challenges like dealing with a difficult roommate, finding the financial aid office and registering for classes requires resiliency and tenacity, and these are two character traits that College Track San Francisco is targeting. The site is working to make habits of mind and GRIT visible to all students by recognizing positive character traits that are linked to college success.

They went a step farther and created a rubric for students that measures the seemingly immeasurable:

College Track Student GRIT Rubric

	Exceeds Expectations	Meets Expectations	Approaching Expectations
Guts: Courageous, bold, and risk-taking			
Academics	• I **am not afraid** to take challenging classes. • I **am always looking** to push myself harder and explore new and different academic opportunities. • I **go above and beyond** in school and at College Track, not just to get grades, but also to learn and challenge myself.	• I **take some challenging** classes and take on new opportunities when I am encouraged to. • I **do what it takes** to get the best grade possible, but that doesn't always mean I challenge myself.	• I **take only the bare minimum classes** in order to graduate, and usually avoid new academic opportunities or challenges. • My goal is **to do what I need to do to pass** with a C.
Leadership	• I thoughtfully **weigh all risks** to think about whether the outcome it will be a net positive or negative, and encourage others to do the same. • I **not only think about** what happens if I *do* take a positive risk, but also consider what might happen **if I don't.** • I **push** my comfort zone and boundaries. While I value the views and feelings of my peers, **my decisions** are my own.	• I **think about** the risks that I am taking, and **consider** the possible outcomes. • I am **interested and enthusiastic** about participating in all events, and am willing to take risks if the results will be positive. • When **making decisions**, I take into account **both** what others may think as well as my own opinions and views.	• I **often act on impulses** and don't think about the risks I am taking or their outcomes before jumping in. • I often **pass up** opportunities and challenges because I put **too much** weight on what my peers think. • I prioritize **others'** views over my **own**.
Resilience: Tough, reflective, and persistent			
Academics	• I **actively look for resources** and support to get through academic struggles without being prompted to. • I **reflect on and understand** my own academic strengths and weaknesses and **actively attempt to find** ways to practice and improve on them. • When I get a low grade or have an academic setback, I **always try** to figure out what I can do better next time!	• I **accept when others offer** resources and support for challenging classes or academic endeavors. • **With guidance, I can reflect** on my academic weaknesses and strengths and how to practice and improve, but don't know how to do this on my own. • When I get a low grade or have an academic setback, **I can bounce back** and don't get overly discouraged.	• I am **unwilling/unable** to accept support to deal with my academic challenges. • I **don't want to reflect** on academic strengths and weaknesses and refuse to try new strategies to practice or improve. • I see low grades or academic setbacks as reflective of my potential, and **I usually get upset** or **give up** as a result.
Leadership	• I **encourage others** to see the positive in their challenges, academic or otherwise. • I **support** my peers by helping them reflect and see their struggles as a chance to learn. • I can **bounce back** from personal setbacks and use my experiences to make better choices.	• I **encourage others** not to give up when they are feeling challenged or struggling. I am sometimes a support for my peers/friends. • I **often bounce back** from personal setbacks and do my best to see them as learning experiences.	• I generally **don't offer support** to my peers when they are struggling or feeling challenged. • When I have a personal setback, it often sends me into a downward spiral, and it's **hard for me to see any positive outcomes** that might come of it.

Continued overleaf

Integrity: Honest, kind and reliable			
Academics	• I **model** academic integrity for other students by actively avoiding of plagiarism, and help other students do the same. • I **always** whole-heartedly accept responsibility for my actions and shortcoming, and I see feedback as a learning opportunity.	• I **show an understanding** of academic integrity by always completing my own work, telling the whole truth always, and following citation guidelines when necessary. • I **usually** accept responsibility for actions and shortcomings and don't feel threatened by critical feedback.	• I general **don't demonstrate** academic integrity; I sometimes take credit for work that is not my own. • I **rarely** accept responsibility for my actions and shortcomings, and I am often threatened by critical feedback.
Leadership	• I **always** promote positive & constructive teamwork by encouraging and supporting the success of not just myself, but also of my peers. • I **consistently** hold myself to the highest standards by always keeping my goals in focus and my community in mind. In addition, I **consistently** acknowledge, value and respect my peers, their communities and their experiences. • I am **always reliable:** I do what I say I am going to do, and always follow through on my commitments/appointments because others are often relying on me. I hold these same expectations for other students and adults in my life.	• I **sometimes** encourage others to do their own best work. When I'm told, I give peers open and honest feedback on their work. • **I usually** present a strong sense of self to others and resist others' negative attitudes. • I am **mostly reliable:** I usually do what I say I am going to do, and almost always follow through on my commitments/appointments.	• I **rarely encourage** my peers to do their own best work, and prefer not to give them feedback. • I **adjust/change my personality** depending on who is watching or what I think others want me to be, or I can be **aggressive and defensive** when others have negative attitudes. • I am often **unreliable:** I tend to miss appointments, or I often don't follow through with my commitments.
Tenacity: Resolved, steadfast, and forward-thinking			
Academics	• I **set ambitious** academic goals and always have a clear understanding of what is needed to achieve them. I am intrinsically motivated by my goals. • I **understand** that progress is more important than perfection, and I am able to see long-term goals as equally important as short-term goals.	• I set **reasonable** academic goals and understand what is needed to achieve them and I see goals as motivational tools. • I **recognize** the importance of long-term goals as well as short-tem goals.	• I **don't set** academic goals, or I do it just as an exercise and not as a self-motivation tool. • I **focus primarily on short-term goals** and I have a hard time to setting and maintaining focus on long-term goals.
Leadership	• I **lead through example** in staying on the path to my goals even though I know there will be obstacles, or things might be slow to change. • I **push** others to meet their goals and **always remain solution-oriented.** • Challenges and setbacks serve as **motivation** for me to come back even **stronger** next time.	• I **actively try** to stay on the path to my goals despite obstacles or slow change. • I remain **solution-oriented** most of the time. • Challenges and setbacks **sometimes motivate** me.	• I **get frustrated** when my progress is slow, and my goals are consistently shifting or changing. • I often **remain focused on the problem** *instead* of the solution. • Challenges and setbacks **often** lead me to **give up** on my goals.

 Special thanks to Lia Izenberg, who developed the GRIT Rubric while employed at College Track

CHAPTER

7

20% Time for Teachers

This chapter details the "Edcamp" movement and how inquiry learning time applies to educators as well. Professional development has changed in the 21st century and 20% Time is a way for teachers to explore the next practices in education, as well as learn from each other. If we expect our students to be curious learners, we need to model this type of intrinsic motivation in our own profession.

Teachers Matter . . .

Research shows that teachers—not books, not technology, not buildings, and not even class size—are the single most powerful driver of student performance. That research is important for two reasons. First, it puts an enormous amount of responsibility and pressure on teachers to drive student success. Second, it should be our guiding priority when we think about how to improve our schools. Better teachers, better students.

This is not a new problem. We've been trying to improve our teachers for the past century of formal education. However, there have been many issues in the current model of professional development for teachers in public, private, and charter schools. Similar to our "industrial" model of education for our students, teachers have had to sit through many "death by PowerPoint" presentations on in-service days.

Simply put, we are still trying to improve teachers' performance through measures that were used 35 years ago. That's not good enough. What made a great teacher in 1980, does not make a great teacher in 2015. If teachers matter, then professional development really matters. Let's first look at what makes a great teacher in today's classroom, in order to figure out what type of professional development will work now and in the future.

What Makes a Teacher Great?

What exactly makes up a great teacher? Is it solely based on how his or her students perform on standardized assessments? Or does it correlate to how successful students are in the next grade level? Further, are we expecting teachers themselves to continue growing and becoming "better" educators through the years?

Currently there are two main models to evaluate teachers. The first, from Robert Marzano, has four domains (that contain 60 elements for teacher growth, development, and performance). The Marzano framework includes:

- Domain 1: Classroom Strategies and Behaviors
- Domain 2: Planning and Preparing
- Domain 3: Reflecting on Teaching
- Domain 4: Collegiality and Professionalism

The Danielson framework is also broken down into four domains, containing 22 components (and 76 smaller elements). As a Pennsylvania teacher, the Danielson framework is used to evaluate throughout the state, and serves as a foundation of teacher effectiveness. It includes:

- Domain 1: Planning and Preparation
- Domain 2: Classroom Environment
- Domain 3: Instruction
- Domain 4: Professional Responsibilities

Figure 7.1 Four Marzano Teacher Evaluation Domains

Did you notice the similarities between the Marzano and Danielson frameworks? Each focuses on only one domain on the actual classroom "instruction." The rest of the domains are about planning, reflecting, and the professional duties of a teacher. While both of these methods can pinpoint how effective teachers are in the classroom, they do not provide a clear roadmap for professional development. Professional development is the next step after evaluating a teacher, but often we fail to make a real effort at improving our current teachers and moving them along the continuum. Danielson argues:

> Multiple measures are needed to help school leaders understand how teaching contributes to student success, because as teachers know, there are no silver bullets in the classroom. Armed with this information, teachers and school leaders can create better professional development programs that promote proven techniques and practices that help students learn, and can make better-informed hiring and tenure decisions.[1]

On the flip side, we have seen budget cuts at all levels of education. Often the first budget item removed is teacher professional development. This includes cutting in-house staff that provide professional development to other teachers, guest speakers and consultants, and even professional time to collaborate and work in tandem with other teachers. In short, traditional professional development is on its last legs.

There are still some schools and institutions that value professional development for staff. Programs like the Verizon Innovative Leadership Schools provide grants to schools specifically for professional development and training. Other grant opportunities are out there, but they are few and far between. Many teachers are faced with new emerging technologies, and a different generation of learners, yet they don't have the resources at their disposal to continue to grow professionally.

Or do they?

The Evolving Teacher (What's Our Role in the 21st Century?)

Scott McLeod is a current Director of Innovation for the Prairie Lakes Area Education Unit after 14 years as an Educational Leadership professor. In pondering our role as educators in the 21st century Scott makes an intriguing point:

> Can anyone else think of an employment sector other than K-12 and postsecondary education where employees have the right to refuse to use technology?
>
> For example, a grocery store checker doesn't get to say "No thanks, I don't think I'll use a register." A stockbroker doesn't get to say, "No thanks, I don't think I'll use a computer." An architect doesn't get to say, "No thanks, I don't think I'll use AutoCAD." But in education, we plead and implore and incentivize but we never seem to require.

> In many industries, knowledge of relevant technologies is a necessary prerequisite for either getting or keeping one's job. Sometimes the organization provides training; sometimes the employee is expected to get it on her own. Either way, the expectation is that use of the relevant technologies is a core condition of employment.[2]

As teachers and educators in the 21st century we need to take ownership of our professional development. Whether it is trying out a new technology, or reading up on the latest research related to the achievement gap, we have to move forward. In a world where everyone is looking for a quick fix, it's essential to change our focus to "growing" better each day and each year, rather than "proving" how good of a teacher we already are.

Principal George Couros has said:

> The *real* game changer in education isn't something external; it is internal. It is the way we think and grow. It is moving from that 'fixed' mindset about teaching and learning, and moving to the 'growth' mindset. It is thinking differently about education and understanding that all of us as people need different things to succeed. To some students, the 'Flipped' model is hugely beneficial, while to some others, gaming is going to push their learning to a new level. Some learn better in isolation, while others excel in collaboration.
>
> There is no single 'thing' that is a game changer. If there was, we would have figured it out and adopted it by now. We have to stop looking for standardized solutions to try and personalize learning. Our mindset towards teaching and learning has to be open to many approaches, not any single one.

Luckily, we have millions of ways to improve as teachers. Some work better than others. Some will push me forward, but may not be good for you. This is where inquiry becomes a key part of professional development. We know what gets us moving as individuals. Do you want to spend your time connecting online, reading journals and educational publications, or maybe attending conferences? Inquiry-based professional development is a way for teachers to explore the next practices in education, as well as learn from each other.

Learn What You Want to Learn: The Story of Edcamp

What if I told you that 20% is not just for students? It's not only for Google or Fortune 500 employees either. We can have the same benefits of 20% Time for teachers through "un-conferences" like Edcamp.

When I first met Kristen Swanson, she was talking at TEDxPhillyEd about the beginnings of Edcamp. Kristen worked right down the road from me, but

I was just getting "connected" online and had only heard rumblings about this "Edcamp Movement."

Kristen grew up a curious kid, creating imaginary worlds with her sister for stuffed animals to live in, taking apart and putting back together different toys, and spending tons of time reading. However, it was her experience in dance class that really led to her path as an educator. Kristen started dancing at the early age of four, and began to take on a few teaching roles as an assistant. She learned more and became a better dancer as she was teaching, while also having a ton of fun. The teaching spark in Kristen had already begun.

Starting her career as an elementary teacher, Kristen began to connect with other teachers around the area and country. Through these connections she began to think about how school should be structured and the role of technology and inquiry in the classroom. Serving as a Technology Director, Kristen responded to a tweet from Kevin Jarrett early one morning asking if anyone would join him at a "BarCamp" the upcoming Saturday. Being a curious learner, Kristen jumped at the opportunity, without knowing what to expect.

After participating in the BarCamp, Kristen and the other educators they met that day were convinced: they had to take this format and use it for education.

Unlike traditional conferences, Edcamp has an agenda that's created by the participants at the start of the event. Instead of one person standing in front of the room talking for an hour, people are encouraged to have discussions and hands-on sessions. Sponsors don't have their own special sessions or tables; all of the space and time are reserved for the things the people there want to talk about. People could pay hundreds of dollars to attend another conference, or they could go to Edcamp for free.

Built on principles of connected and participatory learning, Edcamp strives to bring teachers together to talk about the things that matter most to them: their interests, passions, and questions. Teachers who attend Edcamp can choose to lead sessions on those things that matter, with an expectation that the people in the room will work together to build understanding by sharing their own knowledge and questions.

Close to 500 Edcamps have already been held around the world. This professional development movement is driven by teachers because it is created for teachers. You learn what you want. The power of choice keeps educators coming back, and spreading Edcamps in every corner of the world (even online).

What's interesting about the beginnings of Edcamp is how it started with inquiry. No one told those educators to go to a BarCamp. They weren't even programmers! They were interested in the idea behind a BarCamp, and that interest led to a global professional development movement. The new professional development in education is about choice, and it's filled with curious learners. Edcamp is only one of the many new ways teachers have to learn and grow on their own time.

The New Professional Development

It's Online

I do most of my professional development online. I use social networks like Twitter, Facebook, Pinterest, or Google+ to connect with educators from around the globe. I spend time joining community discussions on Edmodo, Schoology, or other learning management platforms. I take part in online communities like Thinkfinity, Classroom 2.0, Future of Education, and the Educator's PLN. I read other blogs and share on sites like Edublogs and Triberr. The opportunities for online professional development are growing by the day . . . and most of them are extremely fun, not to mention helpful.

It's Anytime

We are living in the "on demand" generation. There are no longer time restrictions on our learning. Consequently, there is no time limit on distractions either. We don't have to "wait" for our favorite TV show to come on. We can watch it "on demand" or DVR it, or find it online. We don't have to wait for our friend to call us back when we are home. We can talk to anyone, or text anyone, at any time. Waiting . . . is almost non-existent in our society. So why should we have to wait to learn something? You have the ability to learn from other educators, so take advantage of it on your own time. Whether it is online, at a local Edcamp, or from a book . . . get started when you are free.

It's with Whoever You Want

This is a big reason I like the new professional development movement like Edcamp and EduCon. The law of two feet is based on a simple premise: "If at any time during our time together you find yourself in any situation where you are neither learning nor contributing, use your two feet; go someplace else." Take that law and apply it everywhere in your learning. Don't stay in situations where you are not adding to the conversation, or learning from the conversation. It's not rude. It's smart. Developing your professional learning network is about learning from those people who interest and inspire you. You can find them in your own school, in your local area, online, and around the world.

It's Based on Your Choice

If this new form of professional learning is online, available at any time, and with whoever you want . . . then it has to be based on your choice. Inquiry is the founding block of innovation. Begin small, by getting online and seeing the opportunities. Talk with a friend or colleague who is already experiencing this type of learning. Ask them where they learn, when they learn, and who they learn with. It's perfectly normal to piggyback on someone else's experiences before jumping in on your own. But once you jump in, make it a point to learn what you want to learn. It will have a snowball effect on your professional development.

Classroom Application: Get Started Now

Connect Online

The first step you need to take is getting connected online. Thousands of teachers connect, share, and collaborate online each day. If you are not yet involved in these conversations, the first place to start is to use what you already use.

Are you a Facebook user? Already on Twitter? Use LinkedIn? Maybe you are on Google+. Each of these social platforms has many teachers just like you, ready to learn and grow. Facebook and LinkedIn have groups of educators that you can join. They are specific (like EdTech in kindergarten) or a bit broader (Literacy Education). Join a group that interests you, watch and learn from the discussion, and then jump in when you have something to share.

Twitter has educators from around the world, talking in real-time. It's an exciting place to share and communicate, and probably has the most teachers active out of the big four social networks. Once you join Twitter, you can search via hashtags for relevant topics that pique your interest. Using the "#" before a word will allow you to search for hashtags. Each hashtag serves as a way for users to talk about the same topic. Search for grade level hashtags (#kinderchat #mschat), subject based hashtags (#engchat #mathchat), or location based chats (#iaedchat #arkchat). You can also search for specific chats like #20time and #geniushour that have to do with inquiry-based learning.

Google+ is a newer social network, but booming with educators. Find Google+ communities that meet your learning needs. Similar to the other social networks, Google+'s communities are based on grade level, subjects, and other educational interests. It's easy to get involved and start sharing.

Build Your PLN

Once you are connected online it's time to build your "Professional Learning Network." This is a commonly used term to refer to the group of people you learn from and with. You'll start to narrow your focus online to topics, subjects, and ideas that best move you forward. Here is when you can start reading blogs, and other publications tailored to your interests.

As you begin to build your professional learning network, the connections will start to become more than just a name. They'll become a person you can learn from and communicate with on a daily/weekly basis. When I first wrote about using 20% Time in my classroom, I had no idea who else was doing similar work in their classrooms. After posting about it on my blog, a number of teachers commented that they were doing similar work with their students. This is how I started to read the blogs of Kevin Brookhouser and Troy Cockrum. Their ideas fueled my ideas.

This exploded with Genius Hour. Now a much larger crew of educators were chatting online about using inquiry-based learning with their students. I was able to learn from them, and share their ideas with my colleagues. This was true exponential growth, and I had found a PLN that both challenged my thinking, and helped me grow.

Take It to Your School

The final piece is taking it to your school. It can seem like a "secret club" to some teachers to connect with others online. But we are doing our colleagues (and our students) a disservice by not bringing these connections to our own buildings.

I struggled at first to share what I was learning online and in Edcamps with my colleagues. I was afraid that they might laugh it off, and say they didn't have time. I started with one conversation. It went well and I had the teacher sign up for Twitter. This led to another conversation, which then led to an in-service. Finally, a year later, I ran an "Edcamp"-style half-day in-service at my school where ten teachers presented sessions and everyone else was able to choose what they wanted to learn. Even the administrators got involved and learned from the staff.

The Big Impact on Your Students

I started this chapter with a simple statement: Teachers matter. They matter because it's their work that can improve student's performance more than anything else. If we want our students to be successful after they've left school, then we must look at improving the profession teacher-by-teacher. The first place we must start in professional development is with ourselves. What are we passionate about? What interests us? What motivates us to keep teaching and growing? For some it may be technology. Others may be interested in literacy. Many have started to flip their classrooms, and gamify the learning experience for their students. What are you doing to improve?

The idea behind 20% Time and inquiry-based learning is that we start learning with a question. It does not only apply to student learning, and innovating in the business world. It applies to growing as a teacher. If we continue to teach the same way every year, it's not only doing our students a disservice, but it is also hurting our profession. I urge you to model inquiry-based learning for your students. Show them what you are learning and how you are learning. You'll get the benefit of improving, and your students will be impacted in how it translates to the classroom experience. Don't wait. Get started now.

Notes

1 www.danielsongroup.org/article.aspx?page=frameworkforteaching.
2 Dangerously Irrelevant, "Right of Refusal" (http://dangerouslyirrelevant.org/2008/01/right-of-refusa.html).

How to Run an Edcamp-Style In-Service at Your School

NOTE: This is slightly different from Edcamp's because some sessions were pre-planned.

Inspiration from Edcamp

I was given the task (as the K–12 Technology Staff Developer) to create a two-hour professional development experience for our high school staff. I say "experience," because that is what it should be . . . Not just a "session" or "presentation." Professional development should be a lasting experience that hopefully inspires and motivates.

Initially I wanted to run an "EdCamp" at our high school (http://edcamp.corg). However, the two-hour time period made it difficult to follow through the exact process of Edcamp and give the appropriate experience. So, I did what any good educator does and tweaked it for my purpose!

The plan was to invite anyone in the staff to lead "conversations" on a topic of their choice. I titled the session "Enhancing Curriculum and Instruction: Let's Learn From Each Other." Once I received my building Principal's blessing, I was off to the races in planning this two-hour in-service.

The Planning Process

First, I planned out how the two hours would flow.

- I would need the first 15–20 minutes to explain what we were going to do, and give a short presentation on "change in education" to set the tone.
- Then the staff would get some sort of map with rooms and the "conversation topics" on it.
- They could choose any three sessions, and each session would last for 20 minutes.
- After rotating three times we would come back to the large room and break out by department to reflect.

Second, I sent out an email to the entire staff three days before the in-service. I did not want to give them too much time to plan, but also needed to know who my conversation leaders were going to be for logistic purposes. The Edcamp model has this happen at the beginning of the day, but this was one of the tweaks I made to have it run for our purpose. Here is the email I sent out:

> Good Morning Everyone,
>
> In preparation for this Friday's in service I want to give you a brief overview of the second session, "Enhancing Curriculum and Instruction: Let's Learn From Each Other."
>
> This session will be run in an "Edcamp" style, where anyone in attendance can be a leader of a conversation. Edcamp is a form of professional development that is garnering support from teachers all over the world due to its inclusive nature of all teachers being leaders. Although we only have 2 hours, I thought it would be a great time for our staff to be able to share how they are enhancing curriculum and improving instruction through the use of technology.
>
> In my role as a staff developer I get to see all of the amazing work teachers are doing every day in this building. I was rarely able to see this as a classroom teacher, and it is something I'm hoping to change. This session is meant to be a way for us to share and talk about what technology is working in our classrooms.
>
> Here is what the two hours will look like:
>
> 9:00–9:20: Overview of the session and a brief introduction to Edcamp conversations and the growth mindset.
> 9:20–9:30: Distribution of map and note-taking sheet.
> 9:30–9:50: Session #1—Find a conversation that interests you and join it.
> 9:50–10:10: Session #2—Find another conversation that interests you and join it.
> 10:10–10:30: Session #3—Find a final conversation that interests you and join it.
> 10:35–10:55: Come back to the Upper Cafeteria and share out what you saw, learned, and discussed in your departments.
>
> So, what do I need from you now? If you are interested in holding a conversation (note: this is not a big presentation, just a roundtable conversation on your experience)—please let me know by the end of the day tomorrow. Those holding conversations will be

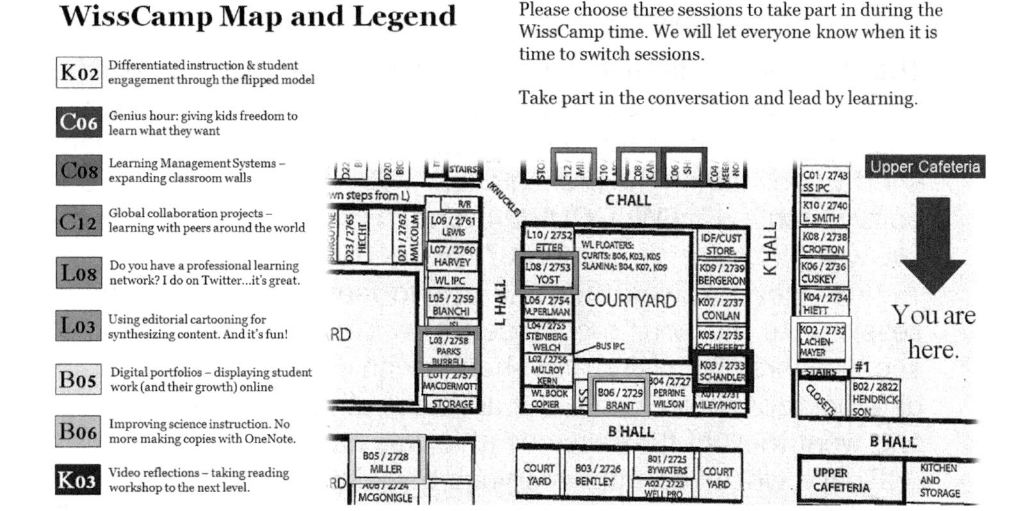

WissCamp Map and Legend

set up in a specific room and lead three 20-minute discussions. Send me a quick note like this:

Conversation Leader(s): Ben Desantis and Rosie Esposito

Topic: Improving math instruction and student engagement through the flipped classroom model

That's it!

I'm looking forward to a great session on Friday. Hopefully you'll be inspired by some of your colleagues as much as I have been this year.

Third, I received eight responses from interested teachers. Many of these teachers had been working with me at some point in time during the year, but others were innovative teachers ready to share a "best or next practice." After talking to some other teachers that day, we settled on nine different sessions (many of which had two teachers co-leading the conversations).

Fourth, I had to get a map set up of where the teachers could host their conversations, and make a quick legend so the traveling teachers could find the right conversations.

Notice that I did not put the conversation leaders' names on the map as I wanted the focus to be on the topic of conversation.

Finally, I sent out a number of emails to the conversation leaders making sure they understood how the day would flow and what was expected of them. They were the best, and really did not need any of my help!

The Day of the In-Service

The staff came in from their first session into the Upper Cafeteria, and I had each person take a map as they signed in. Then I opened up with this presentation (http://tinyurl.com/onm2wnm), and showed two short videos during the presentation—"ProjectGlass" (www.youtube.com/watch?v=9c6W4CCU9M4) and "How to Start a Movement" (www.youtube.com/watch?v=V74AxCqOTvg).

Next they followed the "law of two feet" and went to their first session. As the hour progressed it was great to walk around and see teachers discussing and sharing with each other on a number of different topics and ideas. Our administrative team also participated and went to all of the sessions (this was huge)!

Finally, when I brought everyone back into the cafeteria to debrief I spoke very quickly on the idea of "our mindset as educators." (For more on the topic, see the Education Week article at http://tinyurl.com/pwrbrus.) They had an infographic waiting for them on their tables to look at as I was going over the two different mindsets. The final 10–15 minutes allowed teachers to debrief with each other and share out as a department.

The Final Verdict

The conversation leaders, participants, and administrative team really made this in-service a success. A follow-up survey showed over 88 percent of the staff thought that this in-service was successful. In the comments, teachers were excited to learn from each other, and I received a number of great follow-up emails from the conversation leaders.

What Could We Do Different?

The main gripe with the two-hour in-service was lack of time. Teachers wanted more time to do this type of activity and discuss with each other. Some thought the 20-minute sessions were too short, while others said they liked how it kept moving from session to session. I would love to see how a full day in-service would look with this type of model.

I also urge you to check out the resources at edcamp.org.

CHAPTER

8

Preparing Your Institution, School, and Class

Broken down into three parts, this chapter delves into the preparation, organizing, and implementation stages of running variations of 20% Time. Interviews with school leaders of all levels help shape the need for stakeholders to understand the research and methods behind this type of inquiry-driven education.

Eric Sheninger was a good principal. His school, New Milford High, had a diverse student population and the usual up and down struggles of an American high school. Sheninger made sure his students were focused on school first. His policies didn't allow for cell phones or mobile devices in the building. He was debating blocking YouTube and a variety of other websites that could distract students from their work. His teachers were solid. His curriculum was challenging, yet very typical. In their area of New Jersey, New Milford was looked at as a strong school, but the rest of the country did not care about this school, or its Principal. Then everything changed.

Sheninger became active on Twitter and social media to better reach his stakeholders. While Twitter initially seemed like a waste of time, Sheninger quickly saw the powerful connections that could be made online. He began to see what other schools were doing, not only in the US, but all around the world. Sheninger heard about innovative ways to get students engaged, BYOD (bring your own device) programs, new types of curriculum, and authentic learning experiences.

New Milford soon became a national leader in progressive education. The guiding belief at New Milford High School is that students will find purpose and meaning in their respective learning experiences. Sheninger shared on his blog:

> We have added a series of new courses (19 in just two years), re-written the curriculum of existing courses, made available online courses as part of the VHS Collaborative, and developed numerous authentic learning experiences focusing on the unique interests of our learners. All of these components have become critical elements of the Academies at New

> Milford High School. As a result of these changes and the creation of the Academies, we have seen increases in academic achievement, graduation rates, and acceptances to four-year colleges.

Sheninger is now an award-winning Principal, author, and keynote speaker. In just two years, New Milford went from a good school, to a great school. The students' experience completely changed. Students are not only allowed to bring in mobile devices, they are encouraged to do so as part of a BYOD program. Charging stations litter the hallways, and instruction is fueled by technology. The community is a part of the school and is able to see into the daily activities at New Milford through what is shared online by the staff and students. Educators from all over the country come to visit New Milford and see it in action.

There are so many schools like "New Milford." Schools that have potential to be great, and a chance to change the learning experience. New Milford is not a charter or private school. These students still have to take standardized tests, and the curriculum still has to be tied to state standards. Yet, what New Milford was able to accomplish seems replicable. This is not to say that it doesn't take hard work, a vision, and buy-in from stakeholders. It needs all of those. However, your school can make a transformation to an innovative institution just like New Milford. This chapter looks at the preparation, organization, and implementation of innovative practices at any institution.

Laying the Ground Work

When Eric Sheninger first offered the idea of a Senior Capstone project, teachers at his high school were excited. The idea behind the project was that each senior would get to "choose" his/her final school project, and connect to their passions and interests. While many did not know exactly what the project would look like, they had faith in the process. They had trust in their leader. They had belief in the system.

Too often we find that schools live in a state of fear, rather than a state of exploration. What's interesting, is that fear sometimes drives exploration, but other times it drives people to hide and keep out of the way. Sheninger feared for his current students. He was afraid that they would not be prepared to "create their own journey" once out of high school. His school was a top-performing academic institution, but Sheninger knew that academics could only get you so far. He wanted his students to have what Steve Jobs, Mark Zuckerberg, and Seth Godin all have: drive, grit, and an innovative spark.

His current curriculum didn't allow for seniors to choose their own learning goals. The prototypical "senioritis" had hit his students as well. We prepare these students for 12 years towards a mythical graduation. By January of their senior year they have already applied to colleges, taken all the SATs/ACTs they need to take, and handed in any final transcripts. In reality, they are no longer in school to "achieve" the goal we set out for them, but are really just waiting around for graduation and hopefully staying out of trouble.

This Capstone project gave seniors at New Milford a reason to care. First, it allowed for student choice, which is a serious motivating factor in student engagement and achievement. Second, it was only a pass/fail grade . . . but they were held accountable. More so, they were held accountable because they needed to present in front of their peers. This is the most valuable peer pressure (and also positive). Many were already high achievers on tests and paper, but this was different. This was about creating something that was yours, not doing well on what others were giving to you.

In addition to the Capstone project, New Milford began a new, innovative independent study for students. The "Independent OpenCourseWare Study" (OCW) is selected curricula from outstanding American universities and other institutes of learning, offered free of charge and delivered via the Internet. New Milford's description of the project is as follows:

> This is true authentic learning based on students' passions, interests, and career aspirations. OCW is a twenty-first century phenomenon, a benefit of and testament to the power and global accessibility afforded by the Internet. It is a tool with the potential to improve student achievement by giving high school students a preview of the breadth, scope, complexity, and satisfaction of high quality college classes. IOCS enables high school students to access this powerful learning resource and earn high school credit for their work.

Students are able to complete this independent study by accessing any one of thousands of free courses online by MIT, Harvard, and many other university institutions. Each student enrolls via an online form and moves through the program in a series of checkpoints. The final project has students create a physical product, and present their learning. The rubric is shown in Figure 8.1.

Both the Senior Capstone and the IOCS program are essential to New Milford's position as a 21st-century school. While many of the changes New Milford made were under the direction and guidance of Sheninger, you'll see that they had one thing in common: a focus on the student's learning experience.

If we are to prepare our students for success, our institutions have to fundamentally change. Sometimes a group of teachers can lead this change. Other times a school leader can spark it. If you are reading this book, then you've already taken steps to move your institution forward. But don't do it alone. Get stakeholders involved in the decision-making process, and discuss where your school is now, where you want it to be, and how you can get there by working together.

IOCS Rubric©

	Outstanding (3 points)	Proficient (2 points)	Not Proficient (1 point)
Physical Product	Student uses authentic tools and props to convey new knowledge acquired through specified OpenCourseWare from an approved institution of learning; this can include but is not limited to demonstration of a new skill, learning a new technology; creating a physical model, designing and conducting an experiment, and formulation of a theory.	Student uses some tools or props in addition to a demonstration of knowledge acquired through specified OpenCourseWare from an approved institution of learning in the form of a traditional presentation stemming from specified OpenCourseWare from an approved institution of learning.	Student has lectured on the subject of content from OpenCourseWare from an approved institution, but no physical project is presented other than a PowerPoint, PREZI or other digital presentation tool that contains an abundance of text but lacks depth.
Technology	Student has creatively integrated 2 or more technological tools and/or media resources in the construction of his/her knowledge and development of the final product.	Student has creatively integrated 1 technological tool or media resource in the construction of his/her knowledge and development of the final product.	Student did not integrate any technological tool or media resource in the construction of his/her knowledge and development of the final product.
Depth of Learning	Exposition of learning clearly demonstrates acquisition and application of new knowledge; student is able to answer audience questions and demonstrate extended knowledge; student is likely to be able to apply learning from this project to college and career goals.	Exposition of learning demonstrates some acquisition and application of new knowledge; student may be able to answer some additional questions from audience; student may be able to apply learning from this project to college and career goals.	Exposition does not demonstrate new knowledge. OR The student shows little understanding of the knowledge or skills involved and is unlikely to be able to apply learning from this project to college and career goals.
Public Speaking	Student presented original goals, as well as claims and findings; ideas were sequenced logically and with pertinent descriptions, facts, and details to accentuate main ideas; a concise summarization was provided; there was appropriate eye contact, adequate volume, and clear, correct pronunciation; student showed enthusiasm for this work.	Student presented original goals or claims and findings; ideas were presented with pertinent descriptions, facts, and details to accentuate main ideas; a summarization was provided; student attempted to provide eye contact, adequate volume, and correct pronunciation; student showed enthusiasm for this work.	Presentation lacked one or more of the following: original goals, claims/findings; pertinent descriptions, facts, or details, summarization; appropriate eye contact, adequate volume, and clear, correct pronunciation; may be lacking; student may not have showed enthusiasm for this work.
Studentship	All IOCS directions were followed carefully and forms filled out; all goals outlined at the outset of the project were met and completed on time; presentation was kept within time limits; all forms and feedback requirements were met. All works cited and consulted were presented in correct MLA format.	IOCS directions were generally followed carefully and all forms filled out; some but not all goals were outlined at the outset of the project; specified goals were completed on time; presentation may have been kept within time limits; most or all forms and feedback requirements were met; sources cited and consulted were presented.	One or more of the following is evident: • IOCS directions/forms not carefully followed/filled out • Goals were not outlined at the outset of the project and may not have been completed on time • Presentation not kept within time limits • Forms/feedback requirements not met • Works cited and consulted not presented
Score			

Total Project Score_________**Grade*** _________

Comments____

Figure 8.1

https://sites.google.com/site/opencoursewarestudies/the-iocs-rubric

The Sudbury Valley School

Unlike New Milford, the Sudbury Valley School in Massachusetts is not a public institution. This school is one of the country's first "democratic schools," and has spawned a number of "free schools" that have adopted the name "Sudbury School." You might be wondering: What is a "democratic" and "free" school? Well, unlike the Montessori schools we mentioned earlier, Sudbury schools have no specific guidelines that they follow except one: Every person has a voice in the learning experience.

Adults "work" at the Sudbury schools facilitating learning, but all students create the school rules. Students take part in the lesson planning and teaching process. Regularly held school meetings give the opportunity for anyone in the institution to contribute to the rules, goals, and development of the school. Similarly, there is no specific "grouping" of students. They are free to work in whatever class or age-level they choose. This brings students with shared interests together, and lets inquiry replace age or achievement groupings.

Sudbury schools are also missing something most American schools have: tests. Students choose what they want to learn, and lessons that help them understand a specific concept. They self-assess and judge, while also providing feedback to other students. Adult teachers work alongside students to help throughout this process, but never take it over. This leads to a high level of independent thinking.

Sudbury schools are a complete pedagogical switch from our current public education system. Curriculum is not standard. Teachers are not in charge. Student learning is not assessed through tests. Yet, they've been successful in preparing students and in allowing them to do innovative work while they are still in school. A 1992 alumni survey found that 82% of Sudbury Valley School alumni had graduated from college. Another survey in 2005 showed how successful Sudbury graduates had been, with 90% going on to a formal college education, and many becoming entrepreneurs and business owners.

Mimsy Sadofsky is one of the founders of the Sudbury Valley School. She spoke about the choices students have when they leave the Sudbury school:

> Every student who has wished to has been able to attend college . . . they are going on to college because they want to, not just because it is what many feel is the next step for an eighteen year old. They are going on to higher education, in general, because they have something they want to pursue that is easier to pursue in that setting.[1]

Although this Sudbury type of "un-schooling" can seem radical to most people, it's important to find why it has been successful. This institution is built on a belief that everyone has the potential to do great work regardless of age or ability level. The focus is on growth and helping each person achieve. Much like New Milford, there is an inherent trust built into the institution. Because there is a shared vision, teachers can trust students, students can trust teachers, and parents can trust teachers. That trust makes success possible and replicable.

The Science Leadership Academy

Chris Lehmann is the founding principal of the Science Leadership Academy (SLA) in Philadelphia. SLA is an inquiry-based school that is partnered with the Franklin Institute. Lehmann is an award-winning Principal, author, and education leader who was honored by the White House in 2011 as a "Champion of Change" for education. However, he is also a coach (Ultimate Frisbee), mentor, and lead learner. Lehmann may not be your typical Principal, but SLA is also far from your typical school. Each staff member and student at SLA works towards answering three essential questions:

1. "How do we **learn**?"
2. "What can we **create**?"
3. "What does it mean to **lead**?"

The SLA website puts their mission on display for the entire world to see:

> These three essential questions form the basis of instruction at the Science Leadership Academy (SLA), a Philadelphia high school opened in September 2006. SLA is built on the notion that inquiry is the very first step in the process of learning. Developed in partnership with The Franklin Institute and its commitment to inquiry-based science, SLA provides a rigorous, college-preparatory curriculum with a focus on science, technology, mathematics and entrepreneurship. Students at SLA learn in a project-based environment where the core values of *inquiry, research, collaboration, presentation* and *reflection* are emphasized in all classes.

SLA's focus is on inquiry, research, collaboration, presentation, and reflection. Their students have done amazing work since the school opened, and the school itself has won awards from the likes of Apple and featured in a PBS documentary.

Students take part in an innovative "Individualized Learning Program" (ILP). Every sophomore and junior has to do an internship at a local business, organization, or institution. This learning program allows students to get real-world experience in jobs that interest them and connect to their passions. What better way to prepare students for the "real-world" than to put them right in the middle of it while they are 15, 16, 17 years old.

New Milford and SLA both have seniors complete "Capstone Projects." These projects are often extensions of their ILP Internship experience, and reflect on their personal learning journey at the Science Leadership Academy.

SLA is considered a magnet school in Philadelphia, receiving the same funding from the public school district as other schools. Yet, unlike many schools in the city, it is set up to raise curious learners and innovative creators. Once again we can see the trust in the community for the Principal, the teachers, and the learning process. Whereas the Sudbury school thrives on providing complete freedom to its students, SLA works in the traditional constraints of a public school, but also gives autonomy and ownership to its staff and students.

Different Schools, Different Methods, Same Understanding

Each of these schools are very different in their setup and methods. Each school has a different path to student achievement, and a different story to tell. However, each school is a model of what can happen when inquiry-based learning is supported and embraced.

Preparation

A Shared Vision

Whether this vision comes from the institutional beliefs when it was founded (SLA and Sudbury) or is a new way of thinking about education (New Milford), it is essential that all stakeholders understand the overarching mission. Leaders need to communicate this mission clearly to teachers, parents, students, and community members. When you have a shared vision, the educational experience moves ahead even through tough times and situations.

Movers and Shakers

Every institution needs movers and shakers. These individuals lay the ground work for the rest of the school, and show what can be done. Often, you'll need a few teachers to take on inquiry-based learning before the rest of the school adopts and embraces this shift. When a small group of people can show innovative student work, the rest of the school gets excited. Treat your movers and shakers well, and give them freedom to do great things.

Using Research and Next Practices

This book provides you with a litany of research and resources to support next practices in education. In fact, nothing here is "new." Students have been doing innovative work for centuries, and learners have always learnt best through the inquiry process. However, you will have dissenters and those that want a traditional state of schooling to keep the status quo. They will need research and examples to support change. Give them what they want, and lead by example.

Implementation

It Starts with Trust

One of the key components of any new learning experience is trust. As a coach of a football team, when I call a play my team must trust it is the right call at the right situation. Or else they will question me. However, if they trust me as a leader, then they will never question the call, because they know I am always trying to do what is best for the team. Eric Sheninger and Chris Lehmann have the trust and belief of their stakeholders. Build that same trust by being open and honest in all communication.

What is the Point? Please Let Them Know!

Students and teachers need to know "why" they are doing something. Your vision may be shared, but the path has to be illuminated for all to see. Explain the benefits of an internship program or 20% Time. Share examples of student work from other schools. Tie Genius Hour projects to existing goals and student outcomes. Above all else, make them a part of the process when looking at curriculum and instruction.

Sharing and Reflecting along the Way

There is nothing more powerful than shared reflection. As a community, we can learn so much from each other through our experiences. Classrooms and schools should have time devoted to reflection and sharing. This does not always need to be a presentation. We can learn from the Sudbury model and allow for more multi-grade level collaboration and sharing. As your community shares, it will also grow, and that is what we are trying to accomplish in any educational institution.

Classroom Application: Teachers Can Lead Change Too

Although the examples in this chapter show school leaders as responsible for changing and preparing an institution for this type of change, I firmly believe teachers can lead as well. When I ask teachers why they aren't bringing inquiry into their classroom, I usually get one of two responses:

1. I don't have enough time with my current curriculum.
2. I really have to focus on the standards. How is that going to help my students on the state tests?

So, the dilemma usually unfolds like this: Teacher A wants to bring inquiry into the classroom, but feels they don't have the time in their current curriculum for inquiry, especially when it might take away from instruction tailored to the test. Teacher A also usually worries about the "hoops" they'll need to jump through in order to bring inquiry into their classroom. Do they have to run the idea past their Principal, through the curriculum office, present it to parents? When Teacher A thinks about the benefits versus the pain of doing this type of learning, it's easy to see why they choose to teach the curriculum from the textbook and keep their class moving forward.

On the other side of the hallway Teacher B has been reading some interesting research about the effectiveness of inquiry and project-based learning in the classroom. They stumble across a post from Edutopia that explains the benefits of inquiry-based learning:

> Research shows that such inquiry-based teaching is not so much about seeking the right answer but about developing inquiring minds, and it can yield significant benefits. For example, in the 1995 School Restructuring Study, conducted at the Center on Organization and Restructuring of Schools by Fred Newmann and colleagues at the University of Wisconsin, 2,128 students in 23 schools were found to have significantly higher achievement on challenging tasks when they were taught with inquiry-based teaching, showing that involvement leads to understanding. These practices were found to have a more significant impact on student performance than any other variable, including student background and prior achievement.[2]

Teacher B realized they must begin to implement this type of learning in their classroom for students to succeed right now, and in the future. They take a look at which remote memorization tasks and homework they can replace (not eliminate) from their current curriculum with project-based assessments. They share this information with other colleagues and when their Principal asks questions, they offer up examples of best practices and research.

A growing body of research has shown the following:

1. Students learn more deeply when they can apply classroom-gathered knowledge to real-world problems, and when they take part in projects that require sustained engagement and collaboration.
2. Active-learning practices have a more significant impact on student performance than any other variable, including student background and prior achievement.
3. Students are most successful when they are taught how to learn as well as what to learn.

Let's first understand that the inquiry dilemma in our schools often has to do with lack of research, and a misunderstanding about the benefits of inquiry-based learning. **Genius Hour, 20% Time, and Passion Projects aren't just "fancy" titles for "feel good" school projects. They are real world learning experiences that lead to a strong conceptual understanding of difficult topics and information**.

Do you know any Teacher As that you can enlighten? Are you almost a Teacher B, but are on the edge of getting inquiry started in your classroom? Reach out to those educators that are doing it with students right now in public, private, and charter schools. Join the inquiry movement . . . because we really can't afford not to.

Notes

1 www.sudval.org/essays/122008.shtml.
2 "Powerful Learning: Studies Show Deep Understanding Derives from Collaborative Methods," Brigid Barron and Linda Darling-Hammond on Edutopia (www.edutopia.org/inquiry-project-learning-research).

Institution Checklist

Is your institution ready and prepared for inquiry and innovation? Use this checklist as a simple way to gauge whether or not you are prepared to take the leap:

Check All That Apply to Your Institution

- ☐ Teachers and staff are given time in their schedule to collaborate
- ☐ Teachers and staff connect online through a larger PLN
- ☐ Teachers and staff are routinely updated on new research next practices in their field
- ☐ Teachers and staff have the ability to use technology in the classroom
- ☐ Leaders model effective practice on a daily basis
- ☐ Students are given a variety of "choices" in their learning path
- ☐ Students are provided with collaboration opportunities outside the classroom
- ☐ Students are able to work in "real-world" situations throughout the year
- ☐ Students are assessed in a variety of ways including project-based learning
- ☐ Students are given opportunities to "own" their learning experiences
- ☐ Students produce real work that is publishable, sellable, and/or marketable

CHAPTER

Personalized Learning and the Common Core

Dr. Mitra's "Hole-in-the-Wall" experiment proved that personalized learning experiences can benefit an entire community. However, the Common Core and standards have been seen as inhibitors to inquiry-based personal learning. This chapter delves into the new Common Core and how standards can be applied to personal learning projects like 20% Time.

The Great Communal Experience?

Education is the great communal experience. We go to school (in the US) 182 days a year, for 13 years of our life, and many of us take a much longer educational path. We can discuss similar teachers, extra-curricular activities, lunch-room antics, multiplication tables, algebra troubles, and books. Education, as an American communal experience, is meant in one part to build our national pride, and also to fuel the American dream. We go to school and are taught to expect the best of ourselves, of our families, and our communities. Every child can walk into a school at five years old and come out believing he/she can accomplish anything. This, we say, is what education is all about: It is the bridge between social classes. It eliminates racial misconceptions. It conquers prejudice and bias. It allows anyone, anywhere, to be anything they want to be.

Or so I thought.

As a prospective teacher I had all these grandiose feelings of education wrapped up inside of me. After failing to pick a major during my first two years of being an under-grad, I suddenly had an epiphany: I enjoyed reading. I loved writing. I valued the deeper meaning and critical aspects of literature. I had amazing experiences working with children and teens. I wanted to be an educator.

My Calling to Be in Education

This calling to "make a difference" had been ingrained into me from a variety of life experiences. I grew up in a small suburban town in Pennsylvania. I stayed in the suburban district K-12 and graduated with 36 of my closest friends and peers. For as much as my educational experience was sheltered and confined, my summers were spent visiting other cultures and nations, taking in the diverse political, social, and religious constructs that make each of them so unique. When I was 14 I went on my first of three trips to London to help run a youth group at an after-school community center. I was stationed in Southall, the heavily Muslim, Sikh, and Hindu section of London, and was fascinated by the way such distinct communities of people could live in such close quarters. At 17 I worked with Food for the Hungry in Guatemala. My group built a community center, again held a kids camp, and felt the simultaneous awe and fear of sitting side-by-side complete strangers during an earthquake. The experience helped me realize how emotions and reactions are a universal phenomenon.

I spent two summers in South Africa and Swaziland, volunteering at a medical clinic, running kids camps, preparing a community structure to be used for a medical clinic, church, school, and food shelter. I met 13-year-olds who walked ten miles to school every day, only to walk ten miles back at night to take care of their younger siblings. I saw education as a bridge out of this poverty, but the reality of the situation didn't allow the children there to even know the bridge existed. If there ever was a time where I felt hopeless for education experience, it was during this moment as I came back from my second trip to Africa.

Conversely, as a high school English teacher, I engaged with some of the most impressively bright and talented young people on a daily basis. Many of these skilled individuals will go on to college and be whatever they choose to be, and become successful American stories. But some of these bright and talented young people will, for a variety of reasons, become disengaged from school. Instead of seizing the American dream and using education to go anywhere, be anyone, do anything—they will take it for granted, which in my opinion is worse than never having it at all.

Sugatra Mitra and the Hole-in-the-Wall

Little did I know that during this same time period Dr. Sugatra Mitra, a Chief Scientist at NIIT, was running a Hole-in-the-Wall educational experiment in India. He placed a computer in the middle of an Indian slum, gave it power, and made it accessible with an internet connection. He then sat back and watched how the children in the slum would interact with this new device. Dr. Mitra's premise was simple: Give children access to a computer and internet without any training, supervision, or instructions. Allow them to play and use the device naturally.

With no prior experience, the children were able to use the computer on their own. They did not break the computer. They did not try to steal the computer. And . . . they were learning through the computer's programs and access. This prompted Dr. Mitra to declare the following:

> The acquisition of basic computing skills by any set of children can be achieved through incidental learning provided the learners are given access to a suitable computing facility, with entertaining and motivating content and some minimal (human) guidance.

Dr. Mitra's Hole-in-the-Wall experiment led to significant findings. Students with no teachers, and no prior training or access, could learn incredible amounts of information through the use of one computer. Many asked, "What's the point of having a teacher?" after his results were published, and widely shared TED talk. However, this is not the point.

Dr. Mitra's "learning stations" created a new personal learning model for students of all social backgrounds and environments. The learning station acted as a platform for students to use their natural inquiry and curiosity. A disengaged American student can use a learning station to reinvigorate the learning process as a fun, exciting, and open experience. A third-world student can use the learning station to figure out what makes something work, and discover their local history. In each case, the learning station supports both a personal educational journey, and improves the communal experience.

Dr. Mitra's research found six essential features of the Hole-in-the-Wall Leaning Stations that used a child's natural curiosity to stimulate learning:[1]

1. **Playground Setting:** This is anytime education. The learning station is set up in an open environment so collaboration is natural and all students have access whether they are in or out of school. The unsupervised setting makes it a "learner-centric" setting that sparks curiosity.
2. **Collaborative Learning:** Groups of students can use the learning station at one time, and they'll need to share their experience with other students. This shared learning supports the community and overall group goals of growth.
3. **Optimum Utilization of Learning Station:** Unlike a traditional computer lab, the learning station is not instruction-based. It supports experiential and exploratory types of learning.
4. **Integration with the School System:** Dr. Mitra's research has shown that these stations can support traditional schooling and "reinforces structured learning through peer discussions, increased curiosity and better retention."
5. **Learning to Learn:** Students naturally explore the learning station, and with that comes problem solving and critical thinking.
6. **Projects by Children:** Each learning station can be designed to "engage children in authentic tasks relevant to their daily lives." Instead of merely consuming information at the learning stations, they are set up for students to analyze, synthesize, create, and evaluate. Each of these higher-order thinking skills is embedded into the activities.

Dr. Mitra's experiment and research point to an educational truth: We will learn when given the opportunity. Learning happens regardless of our life experiences, environment, and social position. The learning stations also showed how personal achievement can lead to a communal growth, especially when the community supports the learning process.

Personal Education vs. Communal Education

Through my own personal experiences I realized education meant something different to everyone. Yes, it could be a communal experience where students valued their education and used it as a platform to rise above poverty, social issues, and background. But often education is personal. In fact, it's always a personal journey.

As educators this is a huge shift in thinking. When we see each individual student as a unique educational journey, we begin to understand what growth, achievement, and success look like for that one child.

The communal piece of education is similar to thinking about a team or group. If each student is moving forward with their personal learning journey, then the group will move forward. As the communal group moves forward together, expectations change and new challenges arise.

Inquiry-based learning provides each student with a unique opportunity to improve their skills based on their interests. When we take away inquiry in the classroom, we take away part of the personal journey. We also make it more difficult to share communal success.

Educational standards like the Common Core are often seen as a way to raise the bar and improve the overall communal success of a specific group of people. Most industrialized nations around the world have a set of standards that measure academic achievement and success. International tests like the PISA, have spent years comparing the nations who participate against each other. While I know this is an important measure for international comparison, it often stirs controversy and debate over perceived academic achievement.

Many believe that inquiry-based education cannot exist in a "standard-based" system. However, we've seen an inquiry explosion through 20% projects and Genius Hour projects in the past few years, not only in the United States, but also in Canada, and around the world. Let's look at how standards, like the Common Core, support inquiry and innovation in the classroom.

Enter the Common Core

In Chapter 1 the case is made for a new type of learning experience that prepares our students for life after school, and also gives them the opportunity to create important works during school. Some teachers believe the Common

Core standards restrict this type of thinking, but that is not the case. In fact, the Common Core language is very similar:

> With the growing complexity of the world and the increasing demands of the 21st-century workforce, there is little question that all students should graduate from high school fully prepared for college AND careers.

This quote is taken directly from the standards, and addresses the same issues we are trying to tackle through inquiry-based learning and innovative educational practice. The trouble many teachers, parents, and education leaders have with the standards is their connection to state standardized assessments (which do not allow for inquiry or measure creativity and innovation). I, too, believed standards could be detrimental to the learning process. My belief was centered on the idea that standards made for boring education. I was wrong.

Grant Wiggins and Jay McTighe are the authors of *Understanding by Design* and the accompanying framework for creating curriculum. During their research on the Common Core, they found many educators thought just like I did: Standards were curriculum, and standards supported standardized assessments. Now, there is no denying the fact that high-stakes testing uses standards as a measure of what should be on the assessments, but the Common Core does not dictate a specific curriculum. In essence, we need to reshape our thoughts on what the standards are . . . and what they are not:

> Any set of standards focus on outcomes, not curriculum or instruction. The implication is clear—educators must translate the Standards into an engaging and effective curriculum. So, what is the proper relationship between the Standards and curriculum?
>
> Consider another analogy with home building and renovation: The standards are like the building code. Architects and builders must attend to them but they are not the purpose of the design. The house to be built or renovated is designed to meet the needs of the client in a functional and pleasing manner—while also meeting the building code along the way.[2]

As teachers we need to embrace the role as "builders of the house" and "designers of the learning experience." We cannot use standards as an excuse to not bring inquiry and innovation into our classrooms. Instead, we should be using the standards as a way to support personal learning opportunities and expand the communal experience.

Although the Common Core is in its infancy, there have been a number of studies that link the standards to inquiry and innovation. Let's look at the actual standards. A large quantity of standards specifically tie to inquiry-based learning in some way/shape/form.

Standards that Connect to Reading/Researching with Inquiry

- CCSS.ELA-Literacy.CCRA.R.1 Read closely to determine what the text says explicitly and to make logical inferences from it; cite specific textual evidence when writing or speaking to support conclusions drawn from the text.
- CCSS.ELA-Literacy.CCRA.R.2 Determine central ideas or themes of a text and analyze their development; summarize the key supporting details and ideas.
- CCSS.ELA-Literacy.CCRA.R.3 Analyze how and why individuals, events, or ideas develop and interact over the course of a text.
- CCSS.ELA-Literacy.CCRA.R.6 Assess how point of view or purpose shapes the content and style of a text.
- CCSS.ELA-Literacy.CCRA.R.10 Read and comprehend complex literary and informational texts independently and proficiently.

Standards that Connect to Analyzing and Applying with Inquiry

- CCSS.ELA-Literacy.CCRA.W.7 Conduct short as well as more sustained research projects based on focused questions, demonstrating understanding of the subject under investigation.
- CCSS.ELA-Literacy.CCRA.W.8 Gather relevant information from multiple print and digital sources, assess the credibility and accuracy of each source, and integrate the information while avoiding plagiarism.
- CCSS.ELA-Literacy.CCRA.W.9 Draw evidence from literary or informational texts to support analysis, reflection, and research.
- CCSS.ELA-Literacy.RST.6–8.1 Cite specific textual evidence to support analysis of science and technical texts.

Standards that Connect to Writing and Presenting with Inquiry

- CCSS.ELA-Literacy.CCRA.W.1 Write arguments to support claims in an analysis of substantive topics or texts using valid reasoning and relevant and sufficient evidence.
- CCSS.ELA-Literacy.CCRA.W.2 Write informative/explanatory texts to examine and convey complex ideas and information clearly and accurately through the effective selection, organization, and analysis of content.
- CCSS.ELA-Literacy.CCRA.W.6 Use technology, including the Internet, to produce and publish writing and to interact and collaborate with others.
- CCSS.ELA-Literacy.CCRA.W.10 Write routinely over extended time frames (time for research, reflection, and revision) and shorter time frames (a single sitting or a day or two) for a range of tasks, purposes, and audiences.

- CCSS.ELA-Literacy.CCRA.SL.1 Prepare for and participate effectively in a range of conversations and collaborations with diverse partners, building on others' ideas and expressing their own clearly and persuasively.
- CCSS.ELA-Literacy.CCRA.SL.4 Present information, findings, and supporting evidence such that listeners can follow the line of reasoning and the organization, development, and style are appropriate to task, purpose, and audience.
- CCSS.ELA-Literacy.CCRA.SL.5 Make strategic use of digital media and visual displays of data to express information and enhance understanding of presentations.
- CCSS.ELA-Literacy.CCRA.SL.6 Adapt speech to a variety of contexts and communicative tasks, demonstrating command of formal English when indicated or appropriate.

Standards that Connect to creating and Evaluating with Inquiry

- CCSS.ELA-Literacy.CCRA.R.7 Integrate and evaluate content presented in diverse media and formats, including visually and quantitatively, as well as in words.
- CCSS.ELA-Literacy.CCRA.R.8 Delineate and evaluate the argument and specific claims in a text, including the validity of the reasoning as well as the relevance and sufficiency of the evidence.
- CCSS.ELA-Literacy.CCRA.W.4 Produce clear and coherent writing in which the development, organization, and style are appropriate to task, purpose, and audience.
- CCSS.ELA-Literacy.CCRA.W.6 Use technology, including the Internet, to produce and publish writing and to interact and collaborate with others.
- CCSS.ELA-Literacy.CCRA.SL.3 Evaluate a speaker's point of view, reasoning, and use of evidence and rhetoric.
- CCSS.ELA-Literacy.CCRA.SL.2 Integrate and evaluate information presented in diverse media and formats, including visually, quantitatively, and orally.

Standards for Mathematical Practice

- CCSS.Math.Practice.MP3 Construct viable arguments and critique the reasoning of others. Mathematically proficient students understand and use stated assumptions, definitions, and previously established results in constructing arguments. They make conjectures and build a logical progression of statements to explore the truth of their conjectures. They are able to analyze situations by breaking them into cases, and can recognize and use counterexamples. They justify their conclusions, communicate them to others, and respond to the arguments of others. They reason inductively about data, making plausible arguments that take into account the context from which the data arose.

- CCSS.Math.Practice.MP4 Model with mathematics. Mathematically proficient students can apply the mathematics they know to solve problems arising in everyday life, society, and the workplace. In early grades, this might be as simple as writing an addition equation to describe a situation. In middle grades, a student might apply proportional reasoning to plan a school event or analyze a problem in the community. By high school, a student might use geometry to solve a design problem or use a function to describe how one quantity of interest depends on another. Mathematically proficient students who can apply what they know are comfortable making assumptions and approximations to simplify a complicated situation, realizing that these may need revision later.

As you can see, the Common Core standards and language are specifically tied to a personalized learning experience in which inquiry leads to individual growth. We need to begin "teaching above the test" and using these standards to support inquiry activities in our classrooms, instead of blaming them for a standardized culture.

Taking the Common Experience Farther

If education, as I stated above, is ever going to be the great communal experience, it needs to reach further than ever before. The purpose of education is often debated but I tend to agree with a quote from Bill Beattie:

> The aim of education should be to teach us rather how to think, than what to think—rather to improve our minds, so as to enable us to think for ourselves, than to load the memory with the thoughts of other men.

My education has led me to think many of us are in a position to give hope. This does not mean telling students how to live, or what to do, only "enabling them to think for themselves." I'm eager to make a difference, and that is why I'm here. When you think of what being a great teacher is all about there is another quote I like to reference by William Arthur Ward: "The mediocre teacher tells. The good teacher explains. The superior teacher demonstrates. The great teacher inspires."[3]

Can every teacher be inspirational? Maybe not. But I don't think we all need to be inspirational; instead our classrooms should inspire. Our schools should inspire. And our communal experience should be based around the idea that every personal learning journey matters.

If each student in your class is curious about learning, then your community will be curious. If each student in your class is focused on their personal growth, then your community will respect varying definitions of success. If each student in your class is intrinsically motivated, then your class will inspire each other to do great things every day.

Notes

1 Dr. Sugatra Mitra, "A New Way to Learn" (www.hole-in-the-wall.com/new-way-to-learn.html).
2 "From Common Core to Curriculum: Five Big Ideas," Grant Wiggins and Jay McTighe (http://grantwiggins.files.wordpress.com/2012/09/mctighe_wiggins_final_common_core_standards.pdf).
3 William Arthur Ward "Fountains of Youth".

Common Core Lesson Plan (I-Search Project)

Lesson plan used with permission of Anthony Gabriele

While an I-Search can look different from grade to grade and content to content, the process remains the same. Here is an example of an end of the year project for an 11th grade Advanced Placement Language and Composition course.

I-Search/We-Search Project

"It's so hard when I have to and so easy when I want to." Sondra Barnes

Unit 5: The Rhetoric of Cinema, Documentaries and Modern Media—*Changing the Form*

- How have modes of communication been a reflection of history and society?
- How do modern modes of communication affect the rhetorical devices that individuals have at their disposal?
- How have modern modes of communication been perceived and received by the global community?

Assignment Overview: Working in groups, choose a current form of modern media/rhetoric (*mode of communication*) that you use frequently, are interested in, feel is effective, is beneficial or harmful to society, etc. This should be something that interests YOU. Using this unit's three Essential Questions to guide your research, synthesize the information you find and frame your presentation, develop an argument around your chosen *mode of communication*.

Your project must be technology based and must present itself. You will not be "presenting" these in person, but you will post them for your classmates to see, hear, etc.

*You will also be handing in a "meta-cognitive reflection" on the following:

1. The topic/*mode of communication* (media, rhetoric, etc.) that you chose to present

2. The rhetorical choices YOU made for the mode you decided to use for your presentation

Common Core Standards Addressed

This project can really cover ANY number of the Common Core Standards for Reading, Writing, and Research . . . as well as Speaking and Listening (if the product becomes a presentation along with an essay). Exactly which standards are specifically chosen would depend on the direction the teacher wanted to take the project, as well as what the focus for the mini-lessons would be throughout the unit. Some key standards addressed would be:

Reading informational text (i.e. the material found in research on the Web)

- Key Ideas and Details
  - CCSS.ELA-Literacy.CCRA.R.1
- Integration of Knowledge and Ideas
  - CCSS.ELA-Literacy.CCRA.R.7

Writing—Informative/Explanatory Writing

- CCSS.ELA-Literacy.W.9-10.2
- CCSS.ELA-Literacy.W.9-10.2a
- CCSS.ELA-Literacy.W.9-10.2b
- CCSS.ELA-Literacy.W.9-10.2c
- CCSS.ELA-Literacy.W.9-10.2d
- CCSS.ELA-Literacy.W.9-10.2e
- CCSS.ELA-Literacy.W.9-10.2f

Production and Distribution of Writing

- CCSS.ELA-Literacy.W.9-10.4
- CCSS.ELA-Literacy.W.9-10.5
- CCSS.ELA-Literacy.W.9-10.6

Research to Build and Present Knowledge

- CCSS.ELA-Literacy.W.9-10.7
- CCSS.ELA-Literacy.W.9-10.8
- CCSS.ELA-Literacy.W.9-10.9

Process

Step 1: What am I interested in or passionate about?

Think of a topic (mode of communication) that you are interested in, use on a regular basis, and/or want to explore. Jot it down.

Step 2: Why am I interested in or passionate about this topic?

Introduce your chosen topic and write a paragraph of at least five lines explaining why it is important to you.

Step 3: What do I already know about my topic?

Write a paragraph of at least five lines detailing what you know about your topic—some background or experience you have had.

Step 4: Who can I find to help me understand and expand my topic?

Choose a research partner and share what you have written so far. Be sure to read it out loud; do not just hand your partner your notes! As you share, feel free to elaborate on your written response and add to it.

As a partner, ask questions to help understand the topic completely. Feel free to offer information and advice to help.

Step 5: What questions do I need to generate to guide my research?

Working with a partner, brainstorm a minimum of three questions important to your topic—what do you need to know?

Step 6: Where should I go to find the answers to these questions?

For each question and with your partner, brainstorm where you might find the best answer. Consider primary sources (people, primary source documents), hardcopy sources (magazines, books, newspapers, etc.), and/or electronic sources (on-line sites, blogs, professional and academic databases, key-word searches, focused Google searches, etc.).

Step 7: What are my next steps?

What do you do next? First? What's most important? Do you need to contact someone? Head to the library? Jump on your laptop?) What are your timelines? Can you sort/group your questions to save time in your research? List your steps here . . .

*Now that you have a plan, you can begin to implement it!
**Remember . . . the I-Search process is cyclical and malleable. As the information and your research guide you, be sure to revisit, revise, and re-implement steps as needed!

CHAPTER

10

Taking the Leap into Inquiry

This chapter lays the framework for taking our schools to the next level of inquiry-based education, where all the stakeholders can learn through their passions. When we focus on the students' learning products, instead of them as products themselves (think standardized tests), we can revolutionize the schooling experience.

Project Yesu Comes to Life

In October 2011 Mallory Fundora sat down to write a Christmas list for herself to give to her parents. As she looked around her room she realized there was nothing she needed or really wanted. The more she thought about it, the more she thought about children in Africa, and how they weren't going to get Christmas presents, and there was a lot of things that they needed.

So, Mallory sent her parents an email with a Christmas list, one thing on it: To help Africa. That past August, the Ugandan Orphan Children's Choir came to her church to perform, and she got to meet the children, and they were amazing.

The day after Mallory sent the email to her parents they sat down and talked about what she wanted to do, and how she wanted to help. Mallory contacted Amazima Ministries and Project Have Hope and told them what she wanted to do, and asked them how she could best help them. That is how "Project Yesu" was born.

Mallory talked about the early beginning on her blog:

> My goals at first were simple, but my dream was big. So I started to tell people about Project Yesu, and my mom helped me start a blog so people could read about it. From there it continued to grow. I met my first goal in a week, and by the time Christmas came that first year, I had raised more than I dreamed, and was sponsoring 7 children.

It started with a dream, a desire and bloomed into a passion. Mallory said,

> It changed my life and the lives of people around me. Project Yesu has continued to grow and evolve since starting in 2011. We are constantly looking for areas of need in Uganda, new partnerships to make, and ways to help.

In October of 2012, she traveled to Uganda for the first time. Mallory spent nine days in the country and met her sponsored children. She met their families, visited their homes, and went to their schools. She got to know them, so they weren't strangers or some picture on the internet, they were her kids.

Seeing their schools and their homes made Mallory want to help them even more. When she was walking around their villages, seeing what little they had, it really hit home.

> It made me angry to think about people back in the United States and how we complain about what we have. What surprised me is that the people I met in Uganda, they don't feel sorry for themselves, they don't complain about what they have. They have a joy that is unexplainable. They are the most loving people I have ever met, they are selfless, caring, and welcoming.

Mallory read a famous quote one day from Mahatma Ghandi that said, "Be the change you want to see in the world." It was this type of thinking that sparked her to be a change in the world.

> That's what I want to do, I want to be the change, I want to make a difference, I want to help people. Everyone thinks kids are selfish or that we're just kids and we can't do anything like this. I want to show people what a difference one person can make. If someone, because they heard about me, or met me, decides that they can be a change too, then it will spread from me, to that person, to another person and so on.
>
> Kids have good ideas, and you know what? We don't know all the reasons why it won't work, we just know what we want to do. I know with Project Yesu, I am making a difference, not only in the lives of the children in Uganda who now have food, medicine, and can go to school. But I am making a difference in the lives of my family, my friends, my teachers, and even people I have never met before.

Project Yesu has raised over $15,000 since the end of 2011. Mallory also received the first Bammy Award for Student Initiative at the 2013 Bammy Awards. But more importantly Project Yesu continues to live on and help children in Uganda.

Taking the Leap Together

When I first saw Mallory's story I was inspired. I was also hopeful. Mallory was passionate about something and took the steps to make her dream a reality. Every student may not be passionate about changing the world like Mallory, but they are passionate about something.

Maybe they are passionate about a type of music or band. Maybe they are passionate about a sport. Maybe they are passionate about a specific type of technology. The list could go on. We often dismiss student passions for youthful interests. And maybe part of that is true. The issue comes from never letting them explore what it would be like to live a life based around their passion.

So, what happens is our students stay consumers instead of becoming creators. They play video games instead of making video games. They read comics instead of making comics. They watch reality television instead of filming their own videos. They listen to music instead of writing their own music and lyrics.

Yet we live in a time where you need to create in order to succeed. What is going to separate one student from the thousands of others applying for a job or internship? It's not going to be their grades. It's not going to be what they got on the SAT. It's going to be "what they've done." What a student creates, makes, takes part in, and accomplishes will all be deciding factors for future employment. Furthermore, many of them will have to go down the path of "working for themselves." This is a reality. We need to do a better job of acknowledging this future, and preparing our students for this future.

Mallory didn't do everything by herself. She had help. She had people who valued her ideas, and worked with her to make Project Yesu a success. Teachers need to be that person. We have content knowledge, instructional understanding, and (most importantly) life experience. If all we are doing is taking students through a textbook, then we are failing to help them succeed.

Take the leap into inquiry and innovation with your students. Create opportunities for them to find their purpose and explore their passions. Allow them to fail. And then pick them back up again when they do. Share your failures and experiences with them. Demonstrate an intellectual curiosity by participating in 20% Time or Genius Hour projects. Get parents involved. Take your classroom from a learning space to a maker place. Above all else, do it together.

Maybe you've heard and read about inquiry in the classroom before, and seen it as an abstract concept. Hopefully this book has shown you that inquiry is a powerful learning tool. It's happening in classrooms across the world right now. So, please don't be afraid of inquiry in your classroom. You may give up some control, but in return your student engagement will increase. Students may be covering different standards at different times, but that is a good thing! Inquiry provides content that is always interesting and exciting for each student. That is where we need to start.

Taking the leap with inquiry will also lead to innovation in your classroom. Sometimes we picture innovation as a huge process that is tough to facilitate. However, it's not difficult. It's just different.

Innovation in Education Is Easier than You Think

I've read many different articles and books on the need to "innovate" in education. The authors say similar things: We *need* to use more technology. We *need* to engage students. We *need* to focus on higher-order thinking. Here is the reality.

Some teachers and schools innovate. Most do not.

The teachers and schools that do innovate have it as a part of their culture. They don't spend too much time talking about innovation. They spend time in the trenches making it work.

The teachers and schools who do not innovate like to talk. And debate. And then talk some more. They spend so much time talking about what they should do, and debating the various ways to go about it . . . that they fail to make any progress.

Our educational system is so industrialized that it is hard to not innovate. The problem is when we make "innovation" a huge ordeal. When we have to run innovative ideas past school boards and local committees it gets sticky. When we discuss innovation in department and faculty meetings it becomes an argument. We can't always wait for change and innovation to come from the top down, most of the time we have to make it come from the bottom up. Innovation is easy; take the following examples.

Want Your Students to Become Global learners?

Vicki Davis and Julie Lindsay didn't wait for their school leaders to say, "Let's go global with our students." Instead, they teamed up each of their classrooms to take a look at Thomas Friedman's *The World is Flat* book, and research the ideas together on a Wiki. The technology was available. The connection between the two was decided quickly. And their "Flat Classroom Project" has grown exponentially. They innovated without the curriculum office getting involved.

Pernille Ripp created the Global Read Aloud in 2010 with a simple goal in mind: one book to connect our students across the globe. Since 2010 over 30,000 students and teachers have been connected by reading the same book, sharing their thoughts online, and making connections. No one told Pernille to create the GRA. And no one stopped her when she did.

Want Your School to go 1:1 or BYOD?

Run a pilot in your classroom! Join teachers like Nicholas Provenzano in starting a pilot in your classroom first to show District leaders the benefits of 1:1 or BYOD. Be sure to take great data, and lots of pictures and videos. You can find many grants for technology in the classroom, or try to raise money on DonorsChoose.org.

In my school we wrote a big grant for "Classrooms of the Future" technology. This provided multiple teachers in our district with 1:1 Macbook carts in their class. It eventually led to a full 1:1 program being rolled out.

Having trouble with your school board or administration not understanding how technology impacts and improves learning? Get signed up for BrightBytes. Their quick technology survey (about 10–15 minutes) in Clarity will pull together a full report on where you are strong in technology, and how it is impacting students' and teacher learning.

Want to Change Professional Development in Your School/District?

A group of educators in the Philadelphia area came up with the crazy idea called "Edcamp" after going to a BarCamp (for programmers) and seeing the law-of-two-feet in action. You get to create and pick the sessions to attend and lead. If you aren't feeling it, just walk out and go into another session. There is nothing "formal" about the Edcamp experience, but there is a whole lot of sharing and learning taking place. Thousands of educators will tell you: Edcamp rocks. Last year I ran our very own "WissCamp" with staff at our high school . . . it was awesome. Ten different sessions, and teachers learning from their peers. That's the type of PD I want.

George Couros saw an opportunity this summer to start the "School Admin Virtual Mentorship Program" (#SAVMP). Administration is a challenging job, and many times we get caught up in our district bubble without talking to peers in other places. This program gives the opportunity for "mentors" to work with school leaders in helping them grow as a connected leader. What a great way to model this type of learning for the rest of your staff.

Arin Kress got educators in her district connected by setting up a Skype session with other teachers, students, and Principals around the world (in just three hours)! Her staff was able to talk with educators like Jimmy Casas and Oliver Schinkten about connecting, Twitter, hashtags, and more!

Want to Bring Student Choice Back into a Curriculum Filled with Worksheets?

Gallit Zvi and Hugh McDonald taught together and were always looking for ways to push their students to greatness. One day in 2011 they read a post by Denise Krebs on "Genius Hour" in the classroom. The idea was simple: Give your students time in class to work on a project that they are passionate about. They would research, write, create, and present their Genius Hour project. Both jumped right in, and now have helped inspire hundreds of other "Genius Hour" teachers at the Wiki they set up, and a new collaborative blog. They didn't wait for permission, they just did it.

I started the 20% Project in my classroom because I had a room full of 11th graders who had forgot how fun it was to learn. After running this project, it spread throughout our entire district. We now have 20% Time, or Genius Hour, actually written into our ninth grade ELA curriculum!

Want to Change the Way Students Learn in Your Classroom?

Have you heard of Augmented Reality? If not, it's very cool and easy to use. Two guys with some iPads (also known as Brad Waid and Drew Minock) have put together a nice tutorial: www.twoguysandsomeipads.com/p/meaningful-integration.html on using AR in your classroom and how to get started. I'm planning on using AR for our Parent Conference night. Thanks to these guys, it should be a blast!

Erin Klein threw me for a loop when I saw that she was taking away all the "desks" in her classroom this year. But she did it! Her classroom now looks like a fantastic learning environment, where the kids have multiple learning spaces.

Todd Nesloney is a fifth grade teacher and wanted to do more in the classroom working with students. He chose to "Flip the Classroom" (yes, you can do this with elementary students!). Todd made a great parent letter to send home (in English and Spanish) so that everyone was on the same page. Not only has he made some great videos using the Sophia platform, but his students have made many videos as well.

So, What's My Point?

My point is simple. No one told these people to innovate and improve the education experience for teachers and students. They didn't do it for credit in some class, or for a promotion. Instead, they just went out there and did it. I'm sure each of them had roadblocks and obstacles to overcome. I'm also sure that a few of them may have been called into an "office" to discuss what they were doing. There are thousands of other educators doing innovative work that I didn't mention. They'll keep moving forward this year and in the future.

Get out there and innovate in your classroom and in your school. Make it easy. Make it fun. Make it a better experience for our students.

The Final Step is More Like a Jump

In 2008–2009 a group of students in my tenth grade English class asked the question, "Why do we learn about all of this stuff (genocide and human rights violations), but never do anything about it?" This question sparked an idea and Project: Global Inform (PGI) was created. The students picked their own groups and researched current human rights violations. Each group picked a violation they felt particularly passionate about and began to develop an action plan. Their action plans allowed the students to judge how effective each method of media was at spreading information and creating awareness. At the end of Project: Global Inform's first run, hundreds of people had been met face-to-face with information they did not know, while thousands of other teens and young adults saw videos, visited websites, and became Twitter and Facebook fans of media meant to create awareness.

In 2009–2010 Wissahickon High School took Project: Global Inform to the next level. Over 110 students participated and this time the students were even more creative. In addition to the video, web, and Facebook campaigns—groups began to host events dedicated to raising awareness for their cause. This time, not only was information spread, but money was also raised for organizations currently fighting against human rights violations. Thousands of dollars were raised in just under six weeks, showing that students do have the power to make a difference.

The final step to bringing inquiry and innovation into your classroom can often feel unnatural. It would have been easy for me to give my students a test on human rights violations, and have them write a paper on a specific genocide. The assessment I actually had planned for this unit was a letter to their local government about these atrocities. The students would have learned a little bit about human rights, and then probably moved on.

However, as we've discussed throughout this book, one question changed everything: "Why do we learn about this stuff, but never do anything about it?" I'll always remember that question. It was so simple, yet it stuck with me all night long as I tried to think of a way for my students to "do something" about these human rights violations. I realized that, as a teacher, I had an immense responsibility and power inside of my classroom. My students could go into such depth if I allowed them to, yet I often moved them through the curriculum without taking the time to dig deeper.

This was the first true inquiry project I did with students, and it opened my eyes to what they were able to accomplish. They spent hours putting together campaigns, researching their topic, and spreading awareness across their school and community. The best part: No one complained. Not one student.

At the end of the project each group came up to present what they did, why they did it, and whether or not they felt their campaign was a success. During the action plan stage of the process, each group had listed key benchmarks that would gauge their success. These included goals such as: selling 200 LiveStrong bracelets, having 100 people join our Facebook page, and getting 500 views on our video.

One group came up to present and started off by saying,

> We failed all of our goals. We didn't reach any of our benchmarks, and we wish we had time to do a lot differently. But we learned so much. We had great conversations with our family and friends about the war in Sudan. We learned what it takes to actually sell a wristband (more than you think), and why our strategy didn't work. We realized that working in a team is sometimes difficult, and it's tough when you let other people down. Even though our project bombed . . . we still learned a lot.

That's what this is all about. Let's provide learning experiences for our students, so when they "fail" they still learn. Let's allow our students to choose what they work on so they spend time digging deeper into content and making rich connections. Let's support creative ideas and innovative work, regardless of the outcome. Let's change the way we teach, so students can better succeed.

"Project Global Inform" Unit Plan

Project Description

Human rights' awareness has grown over the past 20 years, but violations still persist, and continue to rise up in the midst of conflict. The 2010 Human Rights Watch Report states that despite the growth in the human rights movement, human rights' defenders remain vulnerable and greatly in need of support by rights-respecting governments (World Report, 2010). The organization's 20th annual review of human rights' practices around the globe summarizes major human rights' trends in more than 90 nations and territories worldwide, reflecting the extensive investigative work carried out in 2009 by Human Rights Watch staff. Executive Director Kenneth Roth argues that the ability of the human rights' movement to exert pressure on behalf of victims has grown enormously in recent years, and that this development has spawned a reaction from abusive governments that grew particularly intense in 2009 (HRW, 2010).

"Project: Global Inform" (PGI) is a peace education project where students use media to spread awareness about human rights' violations. Project Inform came out of the idea that educators too often "teach" students about genocide and human rights' violations, but never "do" anything about it. This project's main objective is to create awareness about current human rights' violations. Which human rights' violations, and what specific actions should be taken, are both the focus and questions of the student's research.

Problem Statement

Currently there is a gap between what students at the secondary and post-secondary levels are learning about human rights' violations, and what is being done to stop them (Cook, 2008). Many humanities' classes and curricula have genocide and human rights as a unit, but assess their students using traditional assessments. This leads to a rote memorization about human rights' violations instead of a true understanding of each situation. Similarly, the organizations fighting human rights have targeted specific violations but lack funding, visibility, and exposure. Students that take part in the fight against genocide and human rights' violations can improve their education/understanding of the world, while helping established organizations get the exposure and funding needed.

Getting Started

PGI can be implemented in a two-, four-, or six-week unit depending on the amount of time a class has to spend on it. Infusing PGI with a current unit/curriculum on genocide and/or human rights violations provides for the best possible experience. PGI has been developed through research of best practices and case studies, and uses experiential learning as the backdrop for successful learning goals and outcomes.

Required Texts

APA Manual, 6th Edition. (2010). Washington, DC: American Psychological Association.

Human Rights Watch (2010). World Report 2010. Retrieved from www.hrw.org/world-report-2010

The Big Picture

Table 10.1

Project Learning Goals: The student will:

- Define peace education and its global ramifications;
- Identify the four roles in any conflict situation (victim, persecutor, bystander, and rescuer);
- Define and apply specific processes of action research;
- Develop an understanding of the methodologies associated with action research that will enable students to:
    - Identify and articulate a problem/purpose statement;
    - List research goals, objectives, and timeline for deliverables;
    - Conduct research and analyze results comparatively;
    - Develop a detailed action plan based on research results;
    - Apply research strategies as a practical problem solving approach in a collaborative setting.
- Use media and technology to create an awareness campaign;

Enduring Understandings:	***Essential Questions:***
• Examine how research project chosen will advance your career; • Identify what you have to offer a potential host organization; • Understand the use of data-driven decision-making process throughout one's career	• What is the relationship between the previous coursework and Co-op research experience? • What kind of Co-op experience is most appropriate to personal & professional growth? • What are the questions/concerns about carrying out the Co-op?

(*Continued*)

Table 10.1 (***Continued***)

Students will know that action research is a process with a variety of approaches and methods. ***Students will be able to*** develop specific oral and writing skills to effectively communicate ideas and research.	
Assessment Evidence	
Authentic Performance Tasks to Demonstrate Understanding:	***Other Evidence Desired:***
• Final Co-op Report • Research Defense	• Reflection journal entries

Project Expectations

Students in this course are expected to be active learners and participants, requiring all students to take an active role in their own learning and to share the learning process with the class. Evidence of active learning includes:

- *Reading and viewing all assigned materials* and making note of questions, areas of interest, and connections you find to other readings.
- *Active participation in Co-op activities* is essential to allow each student to test his or her own assumptions about personal/professional development, as well as expand his/her worldview.
- No assignments will be accepted late.

Handout for Students

Project Summary: Your group will choose a current "human rights' violation" and inform the general public on the issues surrounding the violation. Your task is to create awareness of the violation, because awareness (information) is the first step to taking action. Your group must use technology and media resources to inform, and must create an "action plan" of what, where, when, how, and why you are going to use specific types of media to inform.

Role: Human rights' Activists (Rescuers)

Audience: 1) Your School District; 2) Your Community; 3) Everyone (The General Public)

Purpose: To Inform (Create Awareness)

Task: Use all available resources and technology to inform as many people as possible on a particular human rights violation.

Steps:

1. Research and choose a current Human rights' Violation (use HRW 2010 Report if needed).
2. Create an Action Plan.
3. Use a variety of technologies and media resources to inform the general public.
4. Write a one-page (single spaced) review of the process: outlining the goals, progress, success and failures of your awareness campaign.
5. Present your "awareness campaign" to the class in a five-minute presentation (either live or pre-recorded).

Requirements

1. Create (write) an action plan answering the following questions:
    a. What human rights' violation your group has chosen, and your resources.
    b. Where (online, in-school, out of school, etc.) you are going to inform.
    c. When (specific times/dates, etc.) you are going to inform.
    d. How you are going to create awareness with your chosen media resources.

e. Why you have chosen this violation, and why you have chosen these types of media to inform (why they are the best for the task at hand).

2. Use at least THREE distinct types of media/technological resources to create awareness.
3. You must have a specific "Enduring Understanding" that pertains to your chosen human rights' violation, and focus your information on that understanding. Quality of information is just as important as the quantity of people you reach through the campaign.
4. Be Creative. Be School Appropriate. Work as a Team. Start DOING.

Project Schedule

Table 10.2

Dates	*Topic*	*Readings & Activities*	*Submitted Assignment(s)*
Week I	Understanding Genocide and Human Rights	**Suggested Reading:** 📖 *Night* by Elie Wiesel (and his Nobel Prize acceptance speech)	Reflection Assignment on Darfur Packet
		📖 Sudan/Darfur Packet (can be found on project-inform.org)	Reflection Assignment on "IC: Rough Cut"
		Activity: Watch *Invisible Children: Rough Cut*—Visit Invisible Children.com for more information. Watch collection of "Did You Know" videos on Project-Inform.org. *(Note—These are suggestions. Any reading on genocide and human rights violations is recommended)*	

Week II	Human Rights' Violations (past and present)	**Suggested Reading:** 🕮 HRW 2010 Report 🕮 APA Research Overview	**Write a letter to a state representative on a human rights violation. Assignment is on project-inform.org.**
	Research Methods	Watch "Collected Interviews" and read about past projects' successes and failures on project-inform.org.	
Week III	Developing an Action Plan	**Suggested Reading:** 🕮 Content specific to each groups' chosen human rights' violation	Initial Action Plan turned in following guidelines in the "Action Plan template"
Week IV	Awareness Campaign: Using Media/ Technology Effectively	**Suggested Reading:** 🕮 Content specific to each groups' chosen HRV	**Resubmission of revised Action Plan Campaign work**
Week V	Awareness Campaign: Collecting Data and Measuring Results	**Suggested Reading:** 🕮	Campaign work, Data Collection
Week VI	Written Report and Presentations	**Suggested Reading:** 🕮	Submit final group Report **Present group findings and successes/failures of Awareness Campaign in five-minute presentation**
Post-Project	Reflection		Individual Reflections Post results up on project-inform.org

CHAPTER

11

Support for Inquiry and Innovation in the Classroom

This chapter will shed some light on the research behind 20% Time, and more broadly, inquiry-driven education. The best way to defend inquiry as a practice is to look at the results. It's easy for me to praise 20% Time because I've done it in the classroom, and seen many other teachers do it successfully with their students. However, I also understand that if you have not had that experience it may be difficult to justify. This chapter is for those that need more resources about inquiry-driven education, and for those trying to get research to back them up when bringing it to a Principal, school board, parent committee, or even colleagues.

Since experimenting with 20% Time in my class a few years ago, I've been fascinated by the research and history of this practice in education and the business world. This has led me down a long road to finally writing this book.

During that time I've had hundreds of conversations with fellow teachers practicing 20% Time in some way, shape, or form (Genius Hour, Passion Projects, Choose2Matter, etc). Lately, through the book-writing process I've had some more in-depth interviews about inquiry-based education, and I've spent a great deal of time researching the beginnings and reasons behind 20% Time's effectiveness.

I'm breaking the chapter down into four sections:

1. How inquiry-driven learning increases student engagement and achievement
2. Success-stories from fellow teachers using the inquiry-driven learning model
3. How inquiry-driven learning is connected to the common core standards
4. Related books, whitepapers, and research linked to inquiry-driven education

The Connection between Inquiry and Student Engagement/Achievement

Inquiry Project Learning Research via Edutopia

> Research shows that such inquiry-based teaching is not so much about seeking the right answer but about developing inquiring minds, and it can yield significant benefits. For example, in the 1995 School Restructuring

Study, conducted at the Center on Organization and Restructuring of Schools by Fred Newmann and colleagues at the University of Wisconsin, 2,128 students in 23 schools were found to have significantly higher achievement on challenging tasks when they were taught with inquiry-based teaching, showing that involvement leads to understanding. These practices were found to have a more significant impact on student performance than any other variable, including student background and prior achievement.

(www.edutopia.org/inquiry-project-learning-research)

An Introduction to Inquiry-Based Learning via Neil Stephenson

As contrasted with more traditional forms of teaching and learning, inquiry emphasizes the process of learning in order to develop deep understanding in students in addition to the intended acquisition of content knowledge and skills. Inquiry draws upon constructivist learning theories where understanding is built through the active development of conceptual mental frameworks by the learner. This approach is supported and enhanced by a broad research base which has identified three key implications for effective instructional practices:

1. Students come to the classroom with preconceptions about the world. This means teaching practices must draw out and work with students' pre-existing understandings and make student "thinking" visible and central to the learning.
2. Competence in an area of study requires factual knowledge organized around conceptual frameworks to facilitate knowledge retrieval and application. Classroom activities should be designed to develop understanding through in-depth study of curriculum topics.
3. Meta-cognition (thinking about thinking) helps students take control of their learning. Opportunities for students to define learning goals and monitor their own understanding need to be embedded into classroom tasks.

(http://teachinquiry.com/index/Introduction.html)

The Everyday Classroom Tools Project (Project Zero) via Tina Grotzer and Harvard GSE

The goal of the Everyday Classroom Tools Project is to provide opportunities for students to learn that inquiry and their own experiences can help them achieve a deeper understanding of their world. It aims to foster a spirit of inquiry in all students. These goals promise to help students grow into life-long learners who are curious and set out to seek and achieve deep understanding of the world that they live in.

[. . .]

This document has two sections. The first is a series of six brief essays to address the kinds of questions teachers often have about inquiry-based learning and learning from one's experience. The intent is to place the central concepts of The Everyday Classroom Tools Project in context—to provide a sense of the variety of ways that the concepts have been thought about as well as how they are interpreted in this project. These essays are written for a teacher audience. The second section is a set of big ideas, questions, and attitudes that are central to the project. This section is written with the expectation that teachers will communicate these messages to their students.

(http://hea-www.harvard.edu/ECT/Inquiry/inquiryintro.html)

Why Use Inquiry-Based Learning via Amelia G. Schinck?

An inquiry-based approach was recommended by the National Science Foundation in their 1996 report of a year-long review of the state of undergraduate Science, Mathematics, Engineering and Technology (SME&T) education in the United States entitled Shaping the Future (NSF, 1996). In this report, the researchers stated that it is imperative that: "All students have access to supportive, excellent undergraduate education in science, mathematics, engineering, and technology, and all students learn these subjects by direct experience with the methods and processes of inquiry" (NSF, 1996, p. 6).

(www.inquirybasedlearning.org/?page=Why_Use_IBL)

Hole-in-the-Wall Education Findings from Sugatra Mitra

Over the four-year research phase (2000–2004), HiWEL has extensively studied the impact of Learning Stations on children. Hole-in-the-Wall Learning Stations were installed in diverse settings, the impact of interventions was monitored and data was continually gathered, analyzed and interpreted. Rigorous assessments were conducted to measure academic achievement, behaviour, personality profile, computer literacy, and correlations with socio-economic indicators.

(www.hole-in-the-wall.com/findings.html)

Preparing Students for Work in the 21st Century by Rob Mancabelli and Will Richardson

How can education professionals modify the way they teach and engage students today in order to prepare those students for tomorrow's changing work environments? In part one of this three-part series, education experts Will Richardson and Rob Mancabelli explore the realities of the 21st century workplace. It can be said—without a doubt—that the future world of work for today's students will be vastly different than what we have traditionally prepared these students for. But what implications does this have for today's classrooms?

(http://pages.brightbytes.net/21stCenturyWork_pt1.html)

List of Other Applicable Research on Inquiry-Driven Learning:

- "Evaluating the Use of Inquiry-Based Activities: Do Student and Teacher Behaviors Really Change? Cianciolo, Jennifer; Flory, Luke; Atwell, Jonathan. *Journal of College Science Teaching*", 2006 (http://eric.ed.gov/?q=inquiry&pg=3&id= EJ752661).
- "Inquiry-Based Instruction: Does School Environmental Context Matter?" Pea, Celestine H. *Science Educator,* 2012 (http://eric.ed.gov/?q=inquiry&pg=3&id=EJ977455).
- "How Technology Resources Can Be Used to Represent Personal Inquiry and Support Students' Understanding of It across Contexts." Scanlon, E.; Anastopoulou, S.; Kerawalla, L.; Mulholland, P. *Journal of Computer Assisted Learning,* 2011 (http://eric.ed.gov/?q=inquiry&pg=4&id=EJ943597).

Success Stories of Teachers Using Inquiry-Driven Learning Models

The following is a list of teachers from all levels, principals, professors, and other educators who are currently practicing inquiry-driven education. They write and share their experiences online, and each is a great resource for those getting started.

Angela Maier's Choose2Matter (www.angelamaiers.com)

Angela is an inspiration. Her Choose2Matter Quest and campaign have spread the idea of passion and compassion-based learning far across our country (and the world). Stay tuned for a big way that Choose2Matter will be working with the inquiry-driven community this year.

Cool Cat Teacher Blog (www.coolcatteacher.com)

Vicki Davis is one of the people who really got me moving in the right direction with my students when I started the Flat Classroom Project. Since then I've worked with Vicki on some different projects and have loved what she's been doing with her students. Inquiry is a huge part of Vicki's class and she's one of the best at describing this learning process.

Oliver Schinkten (http://compassionbasedlearning.blogspot.com/2013/06/com-passion-based-learning-next-step.html)

Oliver's Compassion-Based Learning site takes inquiry-driven learning one step further: It's about helping. I love this idea and you can't help but get excited when you read his posts on compassion-based learning.

What's Going on in Mr. Solarz' Class? (http://psolarz.weebly.com/leading-children-to-pursue-their-passions.html)

Paul Solarz does amazing inquiry work with elementary students. If you ever thought, "Oh my students are too young for that," then check out Paul's site and his writing on inquiry and project-based learning in the classroom.

User Generated Education (http://usergeneratededucation.wordpress.com)

Dr. Jackie Gerstein's work with User-Generated Education is highlighted in this blog. She is consistently drawing on resources and research to support user-generated education, including inquiry-driven learning experiences.

Practical Theory (http://practicaltheory.org/blog)

Chris Lehmann is the founding Principal of the Science Leadership Academy (SLA) in Philadelphia, PA. The Science Leadership Academy is an inquiry-driven, project-based, 1:1 laptop school that is considered to be one of the pioneers of the School 2.0 movement nationally and internationally. Chris also is the recipient of ISTE's 2013 Outstanding Leader of the Year award. If you want to see a Principal's perspective on inquiry-based learning, this is the spot!

I Teach. I Think (www.iteachithink.com)

Kevin Brookhouser is someone I greatly respect as a teacher and speaker on inquiry-driven education. He is one of the original folks I know who began doing 20% projects and his blog is filled with great posts and reflections on his (and his students') experiences.

Cogitations of Mr. Cockrum (http://cogitationsofmrcockrum.blogspot.com)

Troy Cockrum is a teacher and author. He is a great teacher to learn from and has also used flipped-learning in conjunction with 20% Time. Last year he participated along with his students in their inquiry-driven project . . . the results speak for themselves!

Kate Petty's: 20 Time in Education (www.20timeineducation.com/20-time-community)

Kate has outdone herself with this site. She has put together resources on getting started with inquiry-driven 20% projects, and has linked to many other teachers doing inquiry-driven learning in their classrooms. Check it out for a much fuller list.

The Nerdy Teacher (www.thenerdyteacher.com)

I was so pumped to see Nicholas Provenzano (ISTE's 2013 Teacher-of-the-Year) starting 20% projects in his class. Nick has been a leader in project-based learning and using Evernote in the classroom. If you want to see someone just starting the inquiry-driven experience, follow Nick's blog this year.

Dare to Care (http://mrsdkrebs.edublogs.org)

Denise Krebs runs Genius Hour (an inquiry-driven project) in her class, and shares what she (and her students) are doing through this blog. It is a must read for those planning on running an inquiry project with middle school students.

My Own Genius Hour (http://geniushour.blogspot.com)

Joy Kirr is a leader online with the #geniushour community and you can always find her giving inspiration to others starting inquiry projects on Twitter (through that hashtag). Joy will tell you that she doesn't do a full "genius hour" but she does allow her students choice and inquiry, which makes all the difference.

Integrating Technology: My Journey (www.gallitzvi.com)

Gallit Zvi is another Genius Hour teacher who consistently inspires. She recently started the Genius Hour collaborative website with Hugh McDonald, where many teachers can cross-share and post their inquiry-driven stories (http://geniushour.ca). Please check it out!

Today Is a Great Day for Learning (http://hughtheteacher.wordpress.com)

Hugh McDonald is a teacher I would want my kids to have! His passion for learning and inquiry is shown on his blog, Twitter, and Instagram feed. Check out what Hugh is doing with his middle school students, and make sure to read the post, "Dear Mr. McDonald, I will never forget Genius Hour."

The Genius Hour Wikispace (http://geniushour.wikispaces.com)

This is another collaborative spot where many teachers are sharing their inquiry-driven learning experiences and resources.

The Global Genius Hour Project Wikispace (https://theglobalgeniushourproject.wikispaces.com)

Robyn Thiessen has set up an amazing site where teachers can come and share what their students are doing with inquiry-based learning in the classroom. You'll find stories of learning from all over the globe, in the entire K-12 age spectrum.

20% Time MOOC: Week #1 Live Class (https://www.youtube.com/watch?v=Rp6zTGyZ0V8)

This MOOC was an awesome learning experience for me this summer. Each week I was able to connect and collaborate with 150 educators about inquiry-driven learning experiences. Please check out this vide which is the first in a series of meeting for the MOOC.

Jesse McLean (http://jessepmclean.com), Josh Stumpenhorst (www.stumpteacher.blogspot.com), Matt Bebbington (http://lookoutforlearning.wordpress.com), and George Couros (http://georgecouros.ca/blog)

Each of these wonderful educators have run "Innovation Days/Weeks" in their schools. It allows the entire school (or grade levels) to use inquiry as a means for inspiring projects for that day/week. I've linked to each of their sites above and you should definitely see what they've been doing!

The Many I Left Off this List

There are many others who have been left off this list, but it is not static! I will update it periodically as I read different blog posts about inquiry-driven learning experiences. For a much longer (and better) list of educators running inquiry projects in their class, check out this Twitter List and LiveBinder put together by Joy Kirr: https://twitter.com/JoyKirr/lists/genius-hour-20-time.

Connection to the Common Core Standards

I wanted to point out the large quantity of standards that already tie to inquiry-based learning in some way/shape/form.

Standards that Connect to Reading/Researching with Inquiry

- CCSS.ELA-Literacy.CCRA.R.1 Read closely to determine what the text says explicitly and to make logical inferences from it; cite specific textual evidence when writing or speaking to support conclusions drawn from the text.
- CCSS.ELA-Literacy.CCRA.R.2 Determine central ideas or themes of a text and analyze their development; summarize the key supporting details and ideas.

- CCSS.ELA-Literacy.CCRA.R.3 Analyze how and why individuals, events, or ideas develop and interact over the course of a text.
- CCSS.ELA-Literacy.CCRA.R.6 Assess how point of view or purpose shapes the content and style of a text.
- CCSS.ELA-Literacy.CCRA.R.10 Read and comprehend complex literary and informational texts independently and proficiently.

Standards that Connect to Analyzing and Applying with Inquiry

- CCSS.ELA-Literacy.CCRA.W.7 Conduct short as well as more sustained research projects based on focused questions, demonstrating understanding of the subject under investigation.
- CCSS.ELA-Literacy.CCRA.W.8 Gather relevant information from multiple print and digital sources, assess the credibility and accuracy of each source, and integrate the information while avoiding plagiarism.
- CCSS.ELA-Literacy.CCRA.W.9 Draw evidence from literary or informational texts to support analysis, reflection, and research.
- CCSS.ELA-Literacy.RST.6-8.1 Cite specific textual evidence to support analysis of science and technical texts.

Standards that Connect to Writing and Presenting with Inquiry

- CCSS.ELA-Literacy.CCRA.W.1 Write arguments to support claims in an analysis of substantive topics or texts using valid reasoning and relevant and sufficient evidence.
- CCSS.ELA-Literacy.CCRA.W.2 Write informative/explanatory texts to examine and convey complex ideas and information clearly and accurately through the effective selection, organization, and analysis of content.
- CCSS.ELA-Literacy.CCRA.W.6 Use technology, including the Internet, to produce and publish writing and to interact and collaborate with others.
- CCSS.ELA-Literacy.CCRA.W.10 Write routinely over extended time frames (time for research, reflection, and revision) and shorter time frames (a single sitting or a day or two) for a range of tasks, purposes, and audiences.
- CCSS.ELA-Literacy.CCRA.SL.1 Prepare for and participate effectively in a range of conversations and collaborations with diverse partners, building on others' ideas and expressing their own clearly and persuasively.
- CCSS.ELA-Literacy.CCRA.SL.4 Present information, findings, and supporting evidence such that listeners can follow the line of reasoning and the organization, development, and style are appropriate to task, purpose, and audience.
- CCSS.ELA-Literacy.CCRA.SL.5 Make strategic use of digital media and visual displays of data to express information and enhance understanding of presentations.

- CCSS.ELA-Literacy.CCRA.SL.6 Adapt speech to a variety of contexts and communicative tasks, demonstrating command of formal English when indicated or appropriate.

Standards that Connect to Creating and Evaluating with Inquiry

- CCSS.ELA-Literacy.CCRA.R.7 Integrate and evaluate content presented in diverse media and formats, including visually and quantitatively, as well as in words.
- CCSS.ELA-Literacy.CCRA.R.8 Delineate and evaluate the argument and specific claims in a text, including the validity of the reasoning as well as the relevance and sufficiency of the evidence.
- CCSS.ELA-Literacy.CCRA.W.4 Produce clear and coherent writing in which the development, organization, and style are appropriate to task, purpose, and audience.
- CCSS.ELA-Literacy.CCRA.W.6 Use technology, including the Internet, to produce and publish writing and to interact and collaborate with others.
- CCSS.ELA-Literacy.CCRA.SL.3 Evaluate a speaker's point of view, reasoning, and use of evidence and rhetoric.
- CCSS.ELA-Literacy.CCRA.SL.2 Integrate and evaluate information presented in diverse media and formats, including visually, quantitatively, and orally.

Standards for Mathematical Practice

- CCSS.Math.Practice.MP3 Construct viable arguments and critique the reasoning of others. Mathematically proficient students understand and use stated assumptions, definitions, and previously established results in constructing arguments. They make conjectures and build a logical progression of statements to explore the truth of their conjectures. They are able to analyze situations by breaking them into cases, and can recognize and use counter-examples. They justify their conclusions, communicate them to others, and respond to the arguments of others.
- CCSS.Math.Practice.MP4 Model with mathematics. Mathematically proficient students can apply the mathematics they know to solve problems arising in everyday life, society, and the workplace.

Other Resources

- P21 Common CoreToolkit: Alighting the CCSS with the Framework for 21st Century Skills (www.p21.org/storage/documents/P21CommonCoreToolkit.pdf)
- PBL and the Common Core (www.thommarkham.com/blog/default/pbl-and-common-core-standards)

Related Books

- *Drive* by Daniel Pink
- *Finding Your Element and The Element* by Sir Ken Robinson
- *The 20% Doctrine* by Ryan Tate
- *World Class Learners* by Yong Zhao
- *Creating Innovators* by Tony Wagner

Related Articles

- "Learning 'to Do' and Learning 'about' Inquiry at the Same Time: Different Outcomes in Valuing the Importance of Various Intellectual Tasks in Planning, Enacting, and Evaluating an Inquiry Curriculum." Syer, Cassidy A.; Chichekian, Tanya; Shore, Bruce M.; Aulls, Mark W. *Instructional Science: An International Journal of the Learning Sciences,* 2013 (http://eric.ed.gov/?q=inquiry&id=EJ999868).
- "The Development of Dynamic Inquiry Performances within an Open Inquiry Setting: A Comparison to Guided Inquiry Setting." Sadeh, Irit; Zion, Michal. *Journal of Research in Science Teaching,* 2009 (http://eric.ed.gov/?q=inquiry&id=EJ867489).
- "Shifting to an Inquiry-Based Experience." Corder, Gregory; Slykhuis, Julie. *Science and Children,* 2011 (http://eric.ed.gov/?q=inquiry&pg=2&id=EJ944172).
- "Connecting Mathematics in Primary Science Inquiry Projects." So, Winnie Wing-mui. *International Journal of Science and Mathematics Education,* 2013 (http://eric.ed.gov/?q=inquiry&pg=3&id=EJ998160).
- "The Practice of Inquiry: A Pedagogical 'Sweet Spot' for Digital Literacy?" Bruce, Bertram C.; Casey, Leo. *Computers in the Schools,* 2012 (http://eric.ed.gov/?q=inquiry&id=EJ963780).
- "The Parallels between Philosophical Inquiry and Scientific Inquiry: Implications for Science Education." Burgh, Gilbert; Nichols, Kim. *Educational Philosophy and Theory,* 2012 (http://eric.ed.gov/?q=inquiry&id=EJ986288).
- "Challenges to Inquiry Teaching and Suggestions for How to Meet Them." Quigley, Cassie; Marshall, Jeff C.; Deaton, Cynthia C. M.; Cook, Michelle P.; Padilla, Michael. *Science Educator,* 2011 (http://eric.ed.gov/?q=inquiry&id=EJ940939).
- "Collaborating to Improve Inquiry-Based Teaching in Elementary Science and Mathematics Methods Courses." Magee, Paula A.; Flessner, Ryan. *Science Education International,* 2012 (http://eric.ed.gov/?q=inquiry&pg=2&id=EJ1001629).

- *Deweyan Inquiry: From Education Theory to Practice.* Johnston, James Scott. SUNY Press, 2009 (http://eric.ed.gov/?q=inquiry&pg=2&id=ED525750).
- "The Benefits of Using Authentic Inquiry within Biotechnology Education." Hanegan, Nikki; Bigler, Amber. *Science Education Review,* 2010 (http://eric.ed.gov/?q=inquiry&pg=2&id=EJ909139).
- "Action Research in Teacher Education: Classroom Inquiry, Reflection, and Data-Driven Decision Making." Eunyoung Hong, Carrie; Lawrence, Salika A. *Journal of Inquiry & Action in Education,* 4(2), 2011 (http://digitalcommons.buffalostate.edu/cgi/viewcontent.cgi?article=1038&context=jiae).
- Concept to Classroom Journal Articles Resources (www.thirteen.org/edonline/concept2class/w6-resources.html#mat).

So, I hope this helps in justifying the use of inquiry-based education, including 20% Time and Genius Hour. Let me know what resources and research I may have missed: I am going to update this list on my website at http://ajjuliani.com/research.

PGMO 06/15/2018